To

Michelle

Just Another Drummer

With Much Love and
Best Wishes,

Thirty Years as an Orchestral Musician

Martin Willis x

20/10/18

Martin Willis

For Conor and Matthew

CONTENTS

Introduction

Firstly, thank you for buying/borrowing/stealing this book.

If you've bought it, you're a wonderful person with obvious good taste, and I thank you again. If you've borrowed it, you've got good taste for a cheapskate, and you're probably a string player and well used to 'borrowing' things, usually from the percussion section like our music stands, chairs, newspapers, etc. If you've nicked it then you're no doubt another fellow drummer without any friends to borrow anything from, so I totally understand and invite you to get in touch so we can compare our empty social diaries.

However you managed to get your hands on it, you're all great.

This is in no way a book on Music history or theory or anything like that.

I'm an orchestral player and although I qualified thirty years ago with a B.A. in Music Performance and a Post-Graduate Certificate in Orchestral Studies, I'm not a Music Scholar by any means. I've always found the playing side of things to be much more fun than discussing the pros and cons of Bartók's use of polymodal chromaticism versus the Serialism of Schoenberg and the Second Viennese School.

I rest my case.

It's also not a memoir along the lines of 'I remember one time I played snare drum with the San Francisco Ballet and I was fabulous at it', even though I did and I was. No-one wants to read self-absorbed stuff like that.

One of the things that gave me impetus to start this project was a throwaway comment from a musician friend that I've known for more than thirty years. It was at a lunch break on a rehearsal day and as we were both walking towards the George Square area of Glasgow, I made a half-joking comment that the morning's conductor was so bad that he'd "made it into the book". I had been toying with the idea of a book at that time but was still a bit unsure of whether I should go ahead with it.

"Are you writing a book?" my friend asked.

"Nah, just a joke," I sort-of lied. "Although I did think about writing a book at one time, a while back," I added, somewhat spontaneously, trying to provoke a reaction.

The reaction I got was quite unexpected. "No offence, but no-one wants to read a book by a 'nobody'".

I live in a small flat in Glasgow and drive a fifteen-year-old Ford which is held together by rust and magic. I'm well aware of my celebrity status or lack thereof and have never once thought of myself as anything other than just another drummer, albeit playing in a slightly more niche genre than most.

I have also read and enjoyed a few books by 'nobodies' and each author has painstakingly stressed their own self-awareness of being as such, and I hope that the same impression will come across in this one.

However, that wasn't what really annoyed me.

It was the defeatist and negative attitude in which it was delivered that got to me, and the fact that the first thing my friend said was a reason why I shouldn't do it.

So, what should I do then? Give up on the idea because they've said that? Just not do anything?

These are attitudes I've always tried to avoid having around me, as I discovered at an early age that their only function is to bring you down to the level of negativity of the speaker and kill any form of creativity or self-challenge immediately and - if you bow to it - with irrevocable finality.

That one comment, however, had the opposite effect of its intended one, and it only served to strengthen my resolve to do something about it and actually start writing.

I do have to admit that it was daunting at the beginning. I hadn't written anything seriously since leaving Music College, apart from one short piece on social media a couple of years ago, an edited version of which I've included in here, later on. It actually did become (mostly) easier once I started though, and as clichéd as it sounds, I've really enjoyed the amazing experience and cathartic process of the whole thing.

And as far as I'm concerned, it has only reinforced the old adage that nothing is impossible.

Nothing.

Maybe it's the years of practice, playing things over and over again until it's acceptable to the standards that I've set myself as a professional musician, and having the mindset that whatever I do could always be improved upon, but I've always absolutely believed that nothing is impossible.

Nothing is unplayable.

Whatever you're aiming for might be difficult to achieve, but if you keep trying and improving, you will eventually and definitely succeed.

If you don't even try, then of course, you may as well just go home and do nothing.

If you try your best - really your best - you will achieve what you set out to achieve.

So please, don't let anyone tell you what you can't do. They are wrong.

If they say something like "No, you can't stick your head in that industrial wood-chipper" or "No, you can't cover yourself in blackcurrant cordial before we visit the wasp farm," then obviously I'd advise going along with that, but otherwise don't let anyone tell you that you're not capable of anything.

I can say this because I've now written a book!

I would never have thought in my wildest imagination that I'd write a book, and my imagination really is pretty damn wild.

And if I can do it, ANYONE can, so if you've ever thought about having a go at it, but were unsure, then just go for it.

Give it a go.

Don't worry that you're a nobody and no-one will read it, because they will. You're reading this just now, so I'll definitely read yours.

A lot has happened over the first thirty years of my career that I believe deserves to be shared with a wider audience and I started to get the first urges to write something down in early 2016, but I didn't actually make a proper start until March 2017.

Everything that follows this is true and it all had an effect on me one way or another, either directly or indirectly.

I wanted to create something that the two loves of my life - my sons - would be able to read later on when they're older and make up their own minds about the things that have happened and appear in this book. Things which helped to make me who I am today and have therefore ultimately had an influence on who they are too.

There's an acknowledgements page at the back, but I have to make a special mention here to Anne Brincourt, one of the finest musicians I've ever met and the most amazing mother to our son. It's extremely rare to have an ex-partner who remains your best friend for years afterwards, and I have had nothing but unwavering support and encouragement (and the odd censure, *almost* always deserved!) and couldn't have completed this without any or all of that.

And so, even though she is fluent in four languages, in her native French - Merci, Anne.

So, to business.

Settle back with a Caipirinha or two and enjoy these stories of professional orchestral life and thoughts from a nobody.

Prologue

It was just before 10am in the last week of August 1984 and as I sat outside room 63, the Percussion Room of the Royal Scottish Academy of Music and Drama, I was fidgeting.

Nervous excitement was taking over as I waited to be called in for my first timpani lesson with my new tutor whom I was about to meet for the first time.

The actual, legendary Martin "Gibbo" Gibson, the Scottish National Orchestra's full-time timpanist would be my timpani teacher for the next four years and it was getting to the point where I really couldn't wait to get this first lesson both started and finished.

I chatted distractedly with a couple of the other percussion students who were hanging around, waiting to quickly grab a marimba and some other percussion gear from the room when the current lesson finished. We'd all been told at our introduction session a couple of days previously - in no uncertain terms - not to interrupt any lesson without good reason and getting instruments from the room wasn't a good reason by any stretch of the imagination.

Without any warning, one half of room 63's heavy wooden double doors opened, the first of two pairs of double doors set three feet apart, thick with soundproofing, and Chris Terian, a fellow first year student also having his inaugural lesson, appeared, closely followed by the timpani tutor who said "Right, who's in next?"

I'd been told that Gibbo always liked to amuse himself by saying something risqué in a new student's first lesson to try and shock them, but no-one would elaborate, not wanting to spoil the "surprise" for me.

I had wanted to ask Chris how his first lesson went, but he didn't stop and disappeared in the direction of the canteen without making eye contact with anyone, so I didn't have a chance. This turned out to be quite unfortunate, as it would have been nice to at least have had a small hint at the impending surprise.

I stood up, picked up my black, cheap plastic briefcase containing my timp sticks, and followed the timpani legend into the room, closing both sets of doors behind me.

Gibbo went over to a small table situated to the side of four Ludwig timpani, sat down and rummaged through a small pile of papers to find the one on which were my details. He gestured to a black hydraulic, height-adjustable stool sitting in the playing position behind the timps.

"Right Martin, sit at the drums and get yourself organised", his London accent just fighting for superiority over another one that I couldn't quite put my finger on.

I opened my stick case and took out my favourites, a pair of medium-soft Paul Finan sticks which I was sure would impress Gibbo to the point where he'd say "Wow, if you're using those sticks then you're obviously brilliant and at a level of greatness that's far beyond anything I can teach you. Let's forget the lesson and go for a beer instead!"

Unfortunately, the pair of mass-produced sticks I now had in my hands, one of which was slightly bent due to being left on a radiator at school six months previously, obviously weren't Gibbo's ideal brand of choice, and I detected a barely concealed sigh of exasperation as he spotted them.

He lit up a Marlborough, blew out a thick cloud of smoke and said "Right, have you got a tuning fork?"

"Yes," I said nervously, "an 'A 440' fork."

"Ok, you only need to say 'A'. Get it out and tune the second top drum to a fifth above it, which would be what note?"

"An 'E'" I said confidently, and thought *hey, this is going pretty well so far!*

I tuned the number three drum to an E and waited on the next instruction.

"Alright, play a roll on the 'E' until I tell you to stop - *mezzo forte*."

I played a roll on the third drum and, in my peripheral vision, I could see Gibbo closely scrutinising my technique for the first of what would turn out to be many times over the following years.

And rather good my roll was too, I thought, considering I was still fairly nervous about the whole thing. I had just left high school after all, and I still felt extremely lucky not only to have been accepted on to the three-year long B.A. Music Performance course, but also to have the opportunity to be taught by a musician of the calibre of the man sitting in front of me right now.

"… Ok, stop."

Here it comes, I thought excitedly. *This is where I learn the secret to perfect technique!*

There was a long pause as he took a draw from his cigarette and slowly blew out another pall of smoke.

"What's wrong?" I asked, looking expectantly at him with a mixture of awe, nerves and imminent beers with the master.

"What hand do you stir your coffee with?"

I must briefly pause here for a moment.

I've changed this phrase from the actual one that Gibbo used, as I've deemed his original a bit TOO risqué, or even *très déplacé,* as the French would say.

If you read that last quoted question and swap the words "stir your coffee" with another single word of your choice, as long as it's a verb pertaining to a certain frenzied, private activity with a sole participant and which is generally considered not to be a good spectator sport, then that will give you the actual sentence.

"Sorry...? What hand do I *what* with?"

"It's the right one, innit? I can tell from your roll. Start using the left one - strengthen that other wrist up!"

So, yes, that was Gibbo's little risqué joke.

As the years went on, I realised that he was actually just trying to be funny but had spectacularly misjudged the sense of humour of most students, or at the very least the level of appropriateness for a teacher-student icebreaker comment.

That opening line aside though, Gibbo turned out to be a rather brilliant teacher and professionally, he has always been a real inspiration to me.

Either way, however, it certainly wasn't what I was expecting as my first piece of advice from my new teacher and it definitely took me by surprise.

Gibbo chortled to himself as he picked up a book of timpani exercises and opened it at the first page.

"Right, Martin, let's start at the beginning…"

And that was my first lesson at Music College, and my introduction to the world of orchestral playing and some of the players who inhabit it.

Chapter One

It's All His Fault

The RSAMD, now called The Royal Conservatoire of Scotland, sits on Renfrew Street in the city centre of Glasgow, and has been there since 1988, purpose-built to house the students belonging to either of the two Schools of Music or Drama from the previous, Georgian-era building on nearby Buchanan Street, which was by 1987 definitely showing its age. I was one of the lucky few students to experience both buildings, as the new one opened in time for my Post-Graduate year.

Established in 1893 to 'provide a source of mental cultivation, moral improvement and delightful recreation to all classes', the Old Athenaeum's school of music developed into the Scottish National Academy of Music in 1929, later becoming the Royal Scottish Academy of Music & Drama[1], and the percussion room was in the centre of the building.

A fairly large, windowless room it was big enough to accommodate two sets of timpani and all the large tuned instruments owned by the Academy, namely marimbas, xylophones, vibraphones, glockenspiels, sets of tubular bells and plenty (although never enough) of storage space for all the other stuff like more glockenspiels, a copious amount of snare drums, cymbals, a few large orchestral bass drums and a plethora of smaller instruments referred to, both lovingly and derogatorily, as "toys".

A few metal cabinets also lined the walls, packed full of sheet music and music theory exercise books alongside books on scales, books on all the different techniques on tuned instruments, techniques on snare drum, rudiments and exercises on snare drum, books of timpani studies, orchestral excerpts for all percussion instruments and was a mini library in itself. A few full-length mirrors were placed around the room, a critical addition to studying one's own body position and technique when practicing solo between lessons.

Because it was windowless and also had a very old, very erratic ventilation system, on teaching days the room was heavy with the smell of cigarettes. A few of us students smoked at the time because, with the naivety of youth, we thought it was cool, although we didn't smoke in the room. However, both Gibbo our timpani tutor and Pam our percussion tutor (who was also Principal Percussion with the Scottish National Orchestra) did, so there was no escaping it and we just had to ignore it and carry on, which was just as well because we spent most of the next three years in it, getting constant headaches from the often-flickering strip lighting combined with the stale air.

By the time the new Renfrew St. building opened, it was actually long overdue as the Buchanan Street building was at the stage where it seemed constantly busy with students, and finding a free practice room was worthy of telling one's friends about it later on in the pub. It wasn't unheard of for students to wait on the ground floor for the lift to take them to the upper floors, and when it arrived only to discover a string quartet practicing in it, having been doing so for hours already, and have to squeeze in beside them.

On the School of music side was the large, rectangular Stevenson Hall which was the main location for most of the concerts at The Academy, as the RSAMD was affectionately known by both students and staff, and the room hosted the whole spectrum of ensembles from symphony orchestra concerts to solo recitals and everything else in between. It was also used for the twice-weekly orchestra rehearsals and functions like charity fund raisers and end of term dances amongst other things.

The School of Drama's main performance venue was the Athenaeum Theatre, the centre feature of the whole building and was more or less constantly in use mainly by the drama side for their plays but also used for operas by the music side. Every December it was also home to the panto, one of the few joint ventures between the two Schools who inhabited the same building, and playing in the band for the panto in my second year was one of the most fun things I was involved in during my time there.

Outside of these productions, the only place in the building students were able to mix with their contemporaries from the other School was the second-floor canteen, situated on the Music side. It was accessible only from the main stairwell which was lined with the names of the great composers, all cast in white plaster with gold painted letters.

And anyway, there was no point in using the lift because it was full of string players.

At the beginning of our time there, we were all young, just out of school and in new and unfamiliar surroundings so everyone stuck to their own groups, and all the usual little cliques quickly formed, but as time went on, the music and drama students began mixing well and I can still remember the bustling canteen vividly and seeing drama students like John Hannah, Robert Carlyle and Alan Cumming to name a few, who would later go on to greater things.

As students though, the natural main focus was on the immediate people close to you and those you spent most time with, which in my case were the other percussion students. Of the five of us who started in first year together, three of us finished the course after three years. One didn't make it past the first year, and the other was my best friend Doug, who had a much better reason for not graduating. That left Chris, whom I've mentioned already, Dave, whom I'll introduce soon and myself.

In 1978, Doug and I were both attending different Primary schools. Doug was at Inchinnan Primary and I was at Rashielea Primary in the new Clydeside town of Erskine, and we had first met when we were both playing football for our respective schools against each other in the primary school's league.

Because Erskine was still in the process of being built and therefore still being populated, there weren't a lot of decent players that the teacher in charge of the school football team could choose from. Frankly, there weren't a lot of actual people he could choose from, so to say that my school's football team wasn't particularly good would be the understatement of the year. Final scores of 12-0 and 13-0 in our opponent's favour weren't uncommon.

At the match in question, on a brilliantly sunny Wednesday afternoon in May, we were playing away to Inchinnan, wearing our new red and white strips which were identical to the Arsenal home strip of the day. In fact, the local paper, the Erskine Gazette came and took a team photo of us kitted out in our new gear that had been supplied by the parents' committee. I still have the cutting of us, posing in team formation and looking like 11 and 12-year-old versions of the 'It Ain't Half Hot Mum' cast. The best thing about the article though, is the one line the paper quoted from the short interview they did with the teacher who was our 'coach', in which he said "Unfortunately the team isn't doing particularly well at the moment." Way to go, coach!

Anyway, I played so well in the first half of the game that I was substituted at half time. I was a bit annoyed with the coach after being taken off, so I wandered down to behind the Inchinnan goal, where I could have the best view of my team mates scoring if, by some bizarre set of circumstances, that were actually to happen or to witness an own goal by the other team which was, in all likelihood the only way we would ever get on the score sheet.

As all the action was up at the opposite end of the pitch as usual, the yellow-jerseyed Inchinnan goalie was leaning against his post and starting to get rigor mortis from the inactivity. We got talking and he told me his name was Dougie and it transpired that we would be going to the same high school after the summer holidays.

"Cool!" I said, "See you then."

A few months later, it turned out we were next to each other alphabetically, his surname being Vipond, and we would be in the same registration class for the next six years. We soon became best friends and I found out that Doug played the drums in the school concert band. I must admit I thought it was a bit weird and somewhat geeky, to be honest but I was slightly impressed all the same. I had loved listening to music ever since I could remember, always trying to imagine what was making all the different sounds on the records and cassettes I listened to from my dad's collection, mainly hits of the Fifties and Sixties, and the likes of The Beatles, Elvis and the Beach Boys, so Doug being able to play an instrument was slightly impressive to me, but really only as a sort of novelty because I didn't know anyone else who played anything.

Towards the end of our first year Doug asked me if I wanted to buy a ticket from him for the school rock band's gig at the end of term. I said "What, and miss a double period of Maths just before lunch? Definitely!"

So, on a hot and sweaty June morning, I followed four hundred and thirty-nine other kids down to the school's 440-seat theatre, with my ticket that I'd paid ten pence for, to see Doug play a concert with the school rock band, "Sorceror". It was during the last two periods before lunch, so obviously it was sold out as everyone wanted to be there, even if they had to pay for it and even if they weren't into rock music either. Most didn't care, as long as they got out of classes.

I was 14 years old, and eighty minutes later my life had changed irrevocably.

I was utterly blown away by the whole experience. I hadn't thought about it beforehand, but that had been my first ever concert. I had just discovered not only rock music but actual live music!

I couldn't take my eyes off of Doug and I had no idea how he could play so amazingly well and make it seem so easy. All the weird/geeky/novelty feelings I'd previously had about the whole drums thing had totally vanished and right then and there I knew that I wanted to be able to do that, more than I'd ever wanted anything else before.

I wanted to play the drums.

And as I still say to this day, it's all Dougie Vipond's fault.

"So how do I go about learning to play?" I asked Doug the next day, and he said "You need to speak to the head of the Music department, Mr Hamilton. He'll sort you out with lessons, but you'll have to start playing in the school concert band and orchestra and stuff."

"I don't mind that," I said, "if it gets me playing the drums! I'll go and see him after school today."

"Make sure you say that you want to play percussion – don't say 'drums'!"

"Ok, thanks Doug. Fingers crossed!" and I left to plan my visit to the music department.

I couldn't wait for the final bell at 3.30pm and I was a bag of nerves as I made my way to the third floor Music classrooms. I went straight to Mr Hamilton's office and, armed with Doug's advice I said, more or less that I would like to play percussion and I'd been wanting to do so for a long time and would there be any chance of joining the school band?

"You want to join the concert band? Excellent!" said Mr Hamilton.

Brilliant! I thought. *This is it! I'm going to be a drummer! Yes! I love you, Mr Hamilton!*

I was so excited! The culmination of the nervous anticipation of what he would say to my request was so great I thought I was going to explode with joy.

That all immediately changed two seconds later, though when he said "We've got enough percussionists, however - we don't need any more."

WHAT?!

"What we do need though, is a trombonist, an E flat horn player and a double bassist. Follow me this way," and he led me, stunned, into quite a large room marked "Instrument Store", filled with metal shelves on which sat a number of hard, black instrument cases of various shapes and sizes, and none of which remotely interested me. "Ok, Martin. Do this…" and with that he pursed his lips together and blew a long raspberry.

I thought, *what the hell is that? And why do I have to do it? Is this some sort of joke?*

I looked at him and realised he was serious.

He must have spotted my confusion because he said "That's how you make a sound on a brass instrument." He must have spotted my confusion again because he explained "E flat horn and trombone are both brass instruments. I want to see if you can make that sound."

"Ah, I see, sir."

Maybe all is not lost, I realised. *If I'm really bad at this he'll have no choice but to take me on as a percussionist!*

I took a deep breath and made the worst sound I possibly could. "*prrrrrphtrrrrrrpht….*another deep breath…. *phpprrrrt… ph…t*".

Ha! Who'd want to hear a trombone that sounded like that? I'm a devious genius!

Mr Keith Hamilton, one of the scariest teachers in the school and undeservedly, in my opinion, known by the pupils to be in those days of corporeal punishment, "a bit leather-happy," due to his perceived penchant for not being afraid to employ The Belt, and not holding back while using it, smiled.

"Brilliant!" He exclaimed. "Here's an E flat horn. Take it home and come back in a few days and tell me how you get on with it."

Man, I was gutted!

I carried the instrument home, almost in tears all the while thinking *No, no, no! This isn't right! How did I end up with this piece of crap?!*

When I got home, I put the thing in a corner and I immediately phoned Doug.

"How did it go?" said the cheery voice on the other end, and I told him what had happened.

"Do you DEFINITELY want to be a drummer?" he asked.

"Yes. Definitely," I said, dejectedly.

"Ok, I'll have a think about it and try to figure something out. See you tomorrow."

The next day at school, Doug appeared with a big smile on his face. "I think I've got a solution!" My face lit up as he said it. "But...."

"But...what?"

I started to sink back into E flat horn depression.

"But it involves you buying my old drum kit for fifty quid and telling Mr H that you've had it for ages and can play it already."

"Won't he ask me to play it in front of him?" I asked.

"I didn't have to when I first told him I played the drums."

"Yeah, but the slight difference there, Doug, was that you COULD actually play the drums!"

"True, but I reckon you'll be ok."

I thought about it for a minute. "Well it seems like it's the only option. I'll speak to my parents about it tonight. Fifty quid... It's a lot of money."

"It's a good wee kit though, Marty - a three-piece!"

"Three-piece? What does that mean?"

"Never mind. Trust me, though - you'll definitely love it. Let me know when you find out from your folks."

21

The upshot was that my parents, two of the kindest people ever to grace the planet, and who would do anything for both myself and my younger sister, Margaret, said yes, they'd buy me Doug's drums although it was a bit out of the blue as they never heard me even mention the word "drums" before.

And so, a couple of days later, I took delivery of a three-piece drum kit. I returned the horn to Mr H. with a bit of truth-bending along the lines of "I think I forgot to mention that I've got a drum kit already" and he said "Oh, you should have said! That's fine then. Bring your sticks to the Junior Band rehearsal tomorrow," without batting an eyelid.

And if he's reading this, he's just found out.

So, all's well that ends well, etc., but to this day I can't look at an E flat horn without getting a little shudder.

Chapter Two

The Boulevard Hotel

Fast forward six years and it's the end of term dance in the Stevenson hall and I'm drunk.

Still standing but definitely drunk, holding a pint glass half full of warm, cheap lager and listening once again to Doug, this time playing with "Gael Force Ten," the RSAMD big band.

It's about 10pm and the room is heaving with people in various stages of sobriety, the vast majority of them RSAMD students, some guests of students, and others who were just the usual Glasgow Friday night revellers passing the building, heard the party going on and had managed to sneak in. Whoever was there would agree though - everyone was having a great time. The drink was flowing, the girls were gorgeous and almost everyone was dancing to the big band, which was in top form and totally blasting the roof off.

As my dancing was more in the style of Thunderbirds, and also the fact that I was only just managing to stand up unaided meant I didn't feel too bad about hanging around near the stage and just listening, all the while trying to slowly dodge the exuberant dancers around me, albeit mostly unsuccessfully.

The band were about twenty seconds into a number - yet another one I didn't know - and I thought I saw Doug trying to get my attention. I looked around me and saw no-one else he would be trying to signal so I looked back at him, pointed to myself and mouthed the word "Me?"

He nodded frantically and motioned with his head for me to come over to him.

I carefully negotiated the small foot-and-a-half high stage in time-honoured drunken fashion and trying my best, and failing, to remain inconspicuous, staggered over to the drum riser and put my head down so I could hear over the noise of the band what he wanted to say.

Just as I did that, Doug immediately stopped playing, stood up and thrust the sticks into my left hand, as my right one had a half-full pint glass in it.

"Carry on playing - I'm dying for a piss!" and quickly ran past me. "We're there," he said hurriedly on his way past, pointing vaguely in the direction of the music stand on which sat the drum kit part, and was gone.

You've got to be kidding me....! I thought, closely followed by a dozen other thoughts all at the same time.

Can't he see I'm too sozzled to walk straight, let alone play anything? But I can't leave them without a drummer.... What should I do?! There are hundreds of people here and I don't even know this number, let alone where we are on the page! No rehearsal and I've never even heard this tune before! Talk about getting dropped right in it! No, I'm not doing it, I'll just sit here until he comes back.

One of the trumpets leaned over to me and shouted "Figure six...NOW!"

Argh!

With a fright, I started playing along tentatively until I could find rehearsal figure six on the kit part, which was really a bit of an impossibility as all the notes I could see on the page had now become a load of big black splodges all randomly and drunkenly jumping about.

Then I had a sudden revelation that filled me with terror.

Hang on a sec... This sounds like the type of number the Buddy Rich Big Band would do... That means there's a bloody drum solo in this one! Doug's done this for a laugh!

Slight panic starts.

A drum solo! Shiiiit! I'm not confident with them at the best of times! What the hell is this going to sound like when I'm so smashed?!

Just then, as I'd suspected, the worst possible thing happened.

The band all stopped and as one, turned and looked at me.

Simultaneously my heart sank and I experienced the feeling in the lower half of my body that one gets as the result of a sudden shock, often eloquently described as "one's arse caving in".

Right, just play anything but do it loudly and with confidence and they won't notice how plastered you are! I told myself.

I started playing anything I could think of, which turned out to be not much more than some loud, random, uneven, terrible fills with a few gaps in between while I tried, in my inebriated state, to remember what I'd just played so I could repeat it again and again.

Doug, this isn't funny! It's been going on for ages now! Not only is it a drum solo but it's a bloody MASSIVE drum solo and I'm rapidly running out of ideas! I'm so gonna kill you later for this!

Just then, one of the alto sax players stood up and signalled to me.

Thank Christ for that! I thought. *Finished at last! Better give them all a clear signal to come back in again...*

"We've stopped!" he shouted angrily. "What the fuck was all that about?!"

I stopped playing, frozen.

Turned out it wasn't a drum solo after all.

I felt a rough tap on my shoulder and turned around to see Doug, with a face like thunder, shaking his head in disbelief and hand outstretched to take his sticks back. We swapped places and he just said "Well done" in the most sarcastic tone ever, as he and the band started the next number and I slinked off, mortified and intent on now drinking as much as I could before the evening finished.

I spent that night in room 63, in total contravention of all the security and fire regulations, wrapped up asleep in a couple of padded timp covers. As I quickly discovered when I kept waking up, freezing and sore during the night, they're not as comfortable as they look and I eventually decided to head home. Home was only three quarters of a mile away but that was obviously way too far to walk the previous evening.

It was now around 7.45am and the Saturday Junior Academy would soon be in full rush hour mode, so feeling absolutely terrible and looking even worse, I left room 63 and immediately bumped into Walter Blair, the Junior Department's Head of Staff.

"Morning, Martin," he chirped. "You're in early!"

I smiled weakly and tried to say "Morning" back to him but all that came out was an unintelligible, hoarse crackle as he zoomed past me.

The next time Doug and I both played kit in the same gig was on this same stage a year later almost to the day, at a Cancer Research fundraiser.

I was playing with Ragamuffin, an original Van Halen-influenced metal band. We used to say that we had quite a following in Glasgow, but looking back now, that was really all just hopeful fantasy I think. We hadn't even recorded anything at that point, never mind released a single.

Our fantastic, lightning-fingered guitarist Matthew Pearce was always surrounded by girls and now plays full time in an excellent metal band called Voodoo Six, and our bassist was the very talented Jimmy Murrison, who would later go on to join Scottish heavyweight rockers Nazareth as their longest-serving lead guitarist. Fronted by the extremely handsome "Diamond" Dave Rousen, also always never without a female on his arm, and myself on drums, usually without a female anywhere near me, we played around the Glasgow area with varying degrees of success and to varying degrees of positive critiques.

We did manage later to record a three-track demo on a reel-to-reel tape that I still have because I put an extra five pounds into the recording fee at the time, but unfortunately nothing on which to play it.

Many bands claim to have played to "twelve people and a dog", a generic term to describe a very small audience to room size ratio, but we actually did.

It was as we pulled up to the front of the Boulevard Hotel in Clydebank in a hired van that I started to get a feeling that something wasn't quite right. The car park was totally empty which was a bit unusual for such a big, popular venue and the actual building itself seemed completely locked up.

"Strange," Jimmy said. He was the only one of us who could drive, so was now doubling as the band's van driver by default.

"Definitely strange," I agreed. "I can't see any advertising either."

Jimmy scanned the area. "Hmmm... you're right. I'll check round the back, see if anyone's about." He disappeared around the back of the whitewashed building and reappeared a couple of minutes later with what looked like someone's great grandmother following slowly behind him.

"I found the owner" he said, nodding in the direction of the old lady who was hunched slightly over with what appeared to be arthritis, and with a look of trepidation said "She forgot we were coming today."

As she unlocked the two huge front storm doors of the hotel for us, Jimmy whispered "And watch out, I think she's a bit grumpy because we've turned up...". We started unloading the van, while she stood just outside the hotel doors, right in our way and forcing us to carry all the heavy gear around her, all the while watching us through narrowed eyes with a mixture of deep suspicion and total disdain.

As Dave and I carried another massive speaker cabinet - the third one so far - around her slight but immovable bent frame, she stared intently at it and then at Dave.

"I hope you're not going to be loud, boys. We can't have it too loud here - I'll pull the plug if it is."

I looked at Dave.

Ruggedly handsome with long bleached-blonde hair, permed in heavy metal-style curls with a skull earring just visible and dangling from his left ear, red spandex trousers held up with a thick white leather studded belt, t-shirt ripped to his stomach, exposing a mass of chest hair and a muscular frame set off nicely by his Miami Vice jacket, sleeves rolled up obligatorily to the elbows and I thought how easy it would be for him to pick her up and insert her head-first into one of the large potted plants sitting in the entrance vestibule just behind her.

He stopped, still holding one end of the speaker and looked at Grumpy, with me supporting the other end and starting to sweat quite a bit, and not just because of the weight I was holding.

She seemed to stare back even more intently at him, challenging him to elicit a response which she could use to cancel the gig there and then, and no doubt have the evening to herself, sitting at her bubbling cauldron, chucking frogs in for a laugh.

Diamond Dave gave her a massive smile.

He was the only one of us who didn't drink and was always immensely charming, which was more often than not rather disarming to those meeting him for the first time and wrongly judging him by the way he dressed. And for us, it was rather funny to watch them squirm uncomfortably when they realised they'd been found out for being a shallow asshole.

"Loud? Us? No way, handsome! We're not loud," he lied, oozing his usual charm. "Will you be coming to the concert, gorgeous?"

We almost wet ourselves.

Old Grumpy had now transformed from being an all-powerful, gig-cancelling, arthritic old witch into a sweet and fragile, Diamond Dave-idolising, arthritic old witch.

"Hee hee," she giggled. "No, I'll be tucked up in bed by then, I'm afraid," and fluttered her eyelashes at Dave.

"Ah shame," he replied, "I'll try not to keep you awake", adding a wink.

"Ooh! Tee hee!" she giggled again and shuffled off into the hotel, eventually disappearing into the kitchen to boil up some eye of newt.

Anyway, that was the last we saw of her, even though we were mega loud that evening.

There had been no advertising for the gig, contrary to what we'd been promised, and there were no guests staying at the hotel, which was obviously becoming more and more of a millstone around the owner's neck as we could see it was starting to lapse into a state of disrepair. Nowadays, though, the hotel is still there but under new management and looking rather fine after undergoing what must have been extensive refurbishment.

I often wonder if they refurbished the ballroom.

The massive ballroom built to hold around five hundred people.

Because of the zero-advertising policy/can't be arsed attitude of the management and because it was situated a bit out of the way if you went by public transport, and it was in the days before mobile phones, the only people who turned up were those whom we'd told by word of mouth.

So, eleven people turned up.

Massive 500-capacity ballroom, eleven people, amps turned up louder than usual to annoy the owner. At least nothing else could go wrong.

Nothing else apart from when I realised I'd forgotten to bring my drum stool and the only solution that would give me close to the height I needed to play was to use three decrepit chairs I found in the deserted bar area, stacked on top of each other.

I was still sitting too low and wobbling all over the place, but four chairs would have been way too high and undoubtedly attracted an unwanted comedy element to our performance. We were a serious band, after all.

We were just over half way through the only cover that we did, the Faces' 'Stay With Me' and had just reached the point where the drums go into an energetic double time one bar before the rest of the band do the same, also widely acknowledged to be the part of the song that makes people say "Ooh! I love this bit!", when a local chap who had been out walking his dog, heard the noise from inside the hotel and had come in to see what was going on, bringing his dog in with him.

I spotted the dog just as we got to that good bit of the song and thought *Haha! A dog!* just as my wobbly tower of chairs decided they'd had enough and gave way underneath me.

I then suddenly experienced the unwanted sensation of dropping unexpectedly down about a foot and a half, which, in turn, caused me to inadvertently catch the leg of my spectacles with my right drumstick and flick/catapult them at speed in a wide arc across the large, dark, almost empty room.

Twelve people and a dog in a massive ballroom and I'm now blind and looking like a midget behind the drums, as only my arms were now visible, and to top it all off, my legs were now bleeding and full of wooden splinters.

At least I was confident that my specs were unlikely to be trodden on by the 'crowd.'

When the song finished, someone came up and silently handed me my specs, expressionless.

"Thanks, man" I said, once again mortified. I put them back on and glanced over at the dog.

It looked back at me with the most bored expression I've ever seen on an animal.

So, as I started to say….

It was a Cancer Research fundraiser in the Stevenson Hall and my band, Ragamuffin were asked to support Doug's band for the evening. Doug had started playing with a small pop outfit called Deacon Blue who were just starting to make a bit of a name for themselves and were steadily building on the small following they already had around Glasgow. The difference between their following and ours was that theirs actually existed, but even so, they played a great set and definitely made a lot of new fans that night too.

In 1987, around three months before our final recitals at the RSAMD and completion of our degree course, Deacon Blue were signed by CBS and Doug made the decision to leave the Academy and not graduate.

At the time, it was a hard choice for him to make and a lot of soul-searching went on before he made his mind up to go with the band, much to the disappointment of our two instrumental tutors, Pam and Gibbo.

Luckily though, as everyone knows now with hindsight, it was definitely the right thing to do, as the band went on to become mega-successful and I'm still very proud of my mate, even in spite of that non-existent drum solo he "made" me play.

Days at the Academy mainly consisted of trying to find a practice space in the building and then trying to take the fullest advantage of it that we could by practicing for hours so that no-one else would nab it, interspersed with our course classes, with the likes of History of Music, Harmony, Theory, Composition and Keyboard Harmony all taking their toll on many students and filling most of us with dread.

We also had to fit in our second study instrument practice and lessons (which was piano for all students except the first-study pianist students, who had to do another second-study instrument, usually voice) and of course, our own first-study lessons.

Everyone had one 1-hour lesson on their first-study instrument every week apart from us percussionists. We had two 1-hour lessons per week, one on timps with Gibbo, and the other lesson on everything else percussion with Pam - snare drum and tuned percussion being the two major disciplines there.

Our first-study part of the course was broken down further into things like the actual instrument lessons, history of percussion, percussion ensemble playing and techniques of teaching, amongst others.

If I had some free time during the morning, I'd be in the second-floor canteen, drinking a worrying amount of coffee that would keep me awake for days, and if it was later in the day I'd usually be in Bogies, the Humphrey Bogart-themed pub next door on Buchanan Street, drinking a worrying amount of anything that would also keep me awake for days.

It was in the canteen one day in September 1986 that one of the drama students approached me as I sat at a table with a few other people and sat down with his coffee.

His name was Robin Begg.

At over six feet tall with blonde wavy hair which was always well styled, a great physique and extremely good looking, Robin had an exuberant and confident personality to match and was always very likeable, I thought.

"Hi Martin, got a minute?" He gave me a huge smile.

"Of course, Robin" I said. "What can I do for you?"

"I'm looking for a drummer. The Drama School's got the Stevenson Hall booked for the end of next month for a Halloween charity concert and I'm getting a band together."

"Cool! I didn't know you played an instrument, mate."

"I don't", he beamed "I'm the singer! I've got the rest of the band sorted already, even the other drummer, and the costume is nearly finished too!" I could tell he was really excited about this.

"Hold on, Robin," I said, slightly confused. "The *other* drummer? Costume? What …"

He cut me off mid-sentence.

"It's a Gary Glitter tribute band! Two drummers on stage at the same time! You'll be drums 1 and little Carl Masson the drama student will be drums 2 and follow you. I'm Gary Glitter!"

"Haha!" I laughed - his enthusiasm was infectious. "That sounds mental, mate - count me in!"

"Awesome, dude! I'll be in touch about rehearsals soon" and with that he stood up and left to brighten some other lucky person's day.

Bearing in mind, it was 1986 and the scandal surrounding Gary Glitter was still about twelve years away. Also, The Glitter Band were a staple fixture in Glasgow at that time, playing a few consecutive nights every December, and very much a part of the Glasgow Christmas vibe, especially amongst the student fraternity.

The gig itself went pretty well and we played all the Glitter hits. I remember Smokey Robinson's "Tears of a Clown" also making an appearance with a guest singer, one of the girls from the drama school who possessed a particularly good voice.

Of the two other main memories I have of the gig, the first is of chewing up a large number of fake blood capsules I'd bought specially for the gig from Tam Shepherd's, the famous joke shop on Queen Street (it was Halloween after all!) and being covered in "blood" for the entire gig. Also, by the end of the evening, so was the Academy's brand new, green Yamaha drum kit that I was using without permission.

Of course, when the heavily blood-stained kit was discovered a few days later by the irate teaching staff, I denied all knowledge of how such a thing could've happened and was just as outraged as they were.

The other fond memory is of the deafening cheer for the unforgettable entrance of Robin, in full Glitter costume, featuring massive silver shoulders which were the centrepiece of his altogether fantastic stage presence throughout the whole gig.

After that night, I didn't really see much of the Glitter band members outside of the canteen, mainly due to our respective extensive course workloads, as it was the final year of study for most of us.

About four or five years later though, I saw an advert on television for milk, probably by the British Milk Marketing Board or some other similar body.

Everything about it gave off an American feel. It was shot in high quality film like a US movie of the time and featured an all-American 1950s-esque Milk Bar and what looked like an all-

American waiter serving milk to some kids, with the advert finishing on a close up of the waiter, still in uniform and enjoying a well-earned glass of milk after a hard day's work, his satisfied grin showing perfect white teeth.

It was Robin!

The ad was on a lot, and if I was in company when it came on, I wasted no time in saying "I played in a band with him!"

The morning after I saw one of these adverts for the umpteenth time, I was heading to a rehearsal with the Scottish National Orchestra and bumped into two of the drama students that I hadn't seen since leaving the Academy, and who were making their way to work at the STV studios for a programme they were involved in.

It was great to see them and we had a brief chat wherein I mentioned the previous night's advert and how good it was to see people even if it was only on the television. They glanced furtively at each other and one of them told me that the milk advert was just about to be pulled as Robin had tragically died in an accident about ten days previously.

I was shocked and devastated, obviously, and more than thirty years later I often still think about him and his film star looks, strutting about the stage and generally just being awesome.

Chapter Three

The Glasgow Apollo

A lot of time was spent at college with another mate, Dave Lyons, a fellow percussion student. We had met when we were both playing in the Strathclyde Schools Orchestra two years previously, and we also met up when we both studied at the Junior RSAMD every Saturday during school term time.

Every day, after we'd done our individual few hours of practice, and sometimes actually instead of doing any practice at all, we'd end up playing snooker for ages to the point that when people asked what we did, we'd say "First study snooker, second study percussion."

One day in December 1984, Dave approached me with a fantastic idea. "Marty, do you fancy busking?" he asked, all excited.

"What? Take a drum kit down Buchanan Street? No thanks, Dave. I'm not carrying a kit anywhere."

"No, no. Not a drum kit - two glockenspiels!"

"Two glocks?" I thought it was another one of Dave's far-fetched ideas, like the one he had about doing a six-man percussion group gig in 'a pub somewhere' and have 'fountains coming out of the xylophone because that would look brilliant'.

"What are we going to play with two bloody glocks, Dave?"

"Christmas carols!" he beamed. "We can use the 'Carols For Choirs' book. I can do the soprano and alto lines, one hand on each and you can do the tenor and bass lines. We'll make a fortune!"

And so we did.

We played mostly down Buchanan Street and along Argyll Street and did indeed make a small fortune, especially the closer it got to

Christmas as people were much more inclined to generosity due to the increased amount of festive alcohol.

And we had a name too: GlockBuskers! - a play on the movie title, "Ghostbusters".

We even got a gig in Littlewoods department store on Cambridge Street, but it only lasted for less than fifteen minutes as, no matter how quietly we played, the combination of the carpeted indoor acoustics, low ceiling and the high metallic frequencies of the two orchestral glockenspiels made it painfully deafening to be anywhere near us and we were both relieved, along with everyone else in the store when the manager eventually stopped us using sign language, as all we could hear by then was a high pitched whine even when we stopped playing.

Dave though, had an eccentric but exasperating habit of borrowing people's sticks and 'forgetting' to put them back after he'd finished with them. If we couldn't find any of our own sticks, the first place we looked was Dave's stick case.

I know he won't mind me saying this, as he's well aware of this little foible and anyway, we all have our own little foibles and no-one's perfect, as they say.

Mind you, he's now with the BBC Scottish Symphony Orchestra and still does it.

Musically, for almost seven years previous to forming the mighty Glockbuskers with Dave, I'd been heavily (no pun intended) into all things Metal, be it Heavy, Progressive, Thrash or any one of a plethora of its sub-genres.

I loved going to Metal concerts, buying huge amounts of LP's, seven-inch singles and latterly CD's and listening to them over and over, with the likes of Queensrÿche, Iron Maiden, Manowar, Black Sabbath, Crimson Glory, Yes, Rush and Dio at the top of my list.

They all received equal playing time when I was at home, alongside most of my collection of NWOBHM - possibly the worst acronym ever invented for any style of music.

It stands for 'New Wave Of British Heavy Metal' and was a phrase coined by music journalist Geoff Barton in 1979 to describe the emergence of Heavy Metal bands during the decline of Punk, and featured such luminaries as Iron Maiden, Judas Priest, Saxon and

Def Leppard. Even Motörhead were included, much to lead singer Lemmy's eternal protestations that they weren't a Metal band at all, but a rock and roll band.

The night before I started the very first day of my first year at the Academy, I went to see Dio play at the famous Glasgow Apollo, supported by a young and as yet unknown Queensrÿche, and was blissfully unaware that it was less than ten months before that iconic venue would close its doors for good.

Dio was an American five-piece band fronted by the legendary Ronnie James Dio, the lead singer with Black Sabbath who took over from Ozzy Osborne and, more importantly is credited for being the inventor of the "rock horns" sign, although it never had a name back then.

I had only left school less than two months before and was there with a couple of pals from my school - Alan Steedman, a year older than me and with whom I shared a flat at that time, and Stephen "Steph" Taylor, a year younger and a fellow Metal-head. One of the school caretakers, Billy, also had a part-time job as a bouncer at the Apollo and had not only got us discounted tickets but had also managed to get us a box to ourselves! Just as the gig was about to start, I caught sight of Diamond Dave in the audience below at the same time that he saw us, up in our box.

"How did you get up there?!" he shouted, green with envy.

"Friends in high places!" Steph shouted back, then, as though he'd just remembered something, turned to Alan and myself and said "I'll be back in a minute!" and dashed out through our private door, his trail of long blonde hair the last bit of him to disappear.

A few minutes later, just as Queensrÿche opened with their first single, "Queen of the Rÿche" Steph reappeared with an unmistakeably self-satisfied look on his face.

"Where did you go?" asked Alan.

"I went to find Billy. He told me earlier to come and see him and he'd have a surprise for us."

Steph paused for what I assumed was dramatic effect.

"Well, what's the surprise, then?" I asked, intrigued.

"Brace yourselves, boys…." He took a deep breath. "I've found out which hotel Dio are staying at! But that's not all… Billy says that we should be able to blag our way in if we get there before the band does!"

I was absolutely ecstatic!

"You're kidding!"

"Nope! It's a small, family-run hotel called 'The Pines' on Park Circus."

Wow! I had been looking forward to this gig for months, and now to have the opportunity to meet my heroes afterwards was just amazing!

We stood for the next couple of hours in our Royal Box, all of us having the best time ever and completely entranced by Dio, and as the band came on to do their first encore, we decided it was time to slip away ahead of the crowds and jump in a taxi to the hotel.

Less than ten minutes later, the taxi dropped us outside the Pines and we took a minute to sort out our battle plan.

The single door to the hotel was one of many in a long line of terraced, very expensive looking buildings and the actual street itself was deserted apart from us - two long haired, tall, skinny metal-heads and a smaller, short haired one standing on the street outside the hotel and arguing, with a lot of 'You go first', 'No, you go first', 'No, you...' going on.

We.... sorry, I mean 'they' eventually decided that I would take the lead and talk our way in as I was really good at that sort of stuff, apparently.

"Ok. There's nobody on the door," I said nervously, "come on, let's go," and we walked as confidently as we could into the deserted lobby of the hotel, looking for a sign to direct us to the bar.

"There!" said Steph, pointing to a sign that read "BAR" with a little arrow pointing downstairs. We descended in semi-darkness, a long single flight of stairs to the lower floor and I spotted an open door to our right, light streaming out into the dim hallway.

Here we go. Don't screw it up now, Marty, I said nervously to myself.

The place was like Doctor Who's Tardis but in reverse.

It had a huge, magnificent exterior that looked on to the street, but got smaller and dingier the further in we went.

I walked through the door and into a little bar area which had about five or six smallish tables dotted about, two of which had been pushed together to form a big table around which sat eight or nine people. They were all guys and girls in their late twenties, all of them dressed similarly to us, but with a slight difference in that they all looked really cool and we three looked like a colour-blind toddler had dressed us.

A thin haze of cigarette smoke filled the room and I approached the bar, forcing myself to smile as nicely as I could at the slightly chubby, laid-back looking guy behind it. He was dressed, not in any bar uniform, but in jeans and a sweaty-looking open necked red checked shirt, which gave me the impression that he was possibly the owner.

"Hi, mate," I smiled, my heart pounding. "Three pints of lager, please."

He eyed me up and down, and I could tell this was going to go one way or the other right now.

"Are you with the band?" he asked in a half growl, without moving his hand in the direction of any pint glass or beer tap.

"Yes," I lied sweetly and smiled even sweeter.

"Ok, no problem. Here you go," and he immediately changed into the most helpful chap ever, as he put three beers on the counter for us and couldn't do enough for everyone for the rest of the evening.

The only other people in the room - the group at the big table, whom I'd noticed had done the wild west saloon silent thing as we entered and had been watching us very obviously lie our way into the place - started chatting again amongst themselves, the chance of the entertainment of our possible ejection having now vanished.

The three of us stood at the bar, nerves shot to bits as we finished our drinks in record time, each of us with a satisfied sigh of relief that we'd actually made it in.

"Jesus, that was scary!" Steph said under his breath.

"I know," I whispered back. "That's the last time I'm listening to you two…"

Suddenly, one of the guys from the big group shouted over to us. "Hey, guys! Don't just stand over there - come over here!" and there was a lot of shuffling about as they made room for us to sit with them, so we went over and joined them.

"Thanks very much, mate," I said to the guy who'd shouted us over.

As I got closer, I thought I recognised him and was pretty sure I'd seen him before.

"I'm Martin. Have we met?" I asked him.

"Mick," he grinned, and shook my hand. "Nah, I don't think we've met, Martin. I would've remembered."

As we started chatting, I realised that I recognised all the guys sitting at the table and it slowly dawned on me who they were, just as Steph leaned over to me and surreptitiously whispered "It's 'Glasgow'!"

It was indeed the Glasgow-based Metal band, 'Glasgow'!

They were famous!

In Glasgow! (And also, Japan!)

"Mick Boyle! Glasgow!" I said a bit too excitedly. "That's how I know you!"

"Haha, yes that's us."

They were all really nice people, every one of them and their girlfriends, and we had a great chat for almost an hour before the first Dio band member arrived. Mick told me he was excited about meeting the rock god that was Ronnie James Dio, and I thought it was really nice to hear that big stars like Mick still felt like that sometimes, and it made him all the more likeable too. He asked me if I was looking forward to meeting anyone in particular from the band.

"Yes, of course! I can't wait to meet all of them, but especially Vinnie!" I said, with an approving nod from Mick. "I've already worked out what I'm going to say to him too. He's gonna think I'm so amazing when I say it, and he'll want to spend the rest of the evening chatting with only me, and all you lot will be so jealous!" I was saying it jokingly, but deep down I did think that this might be true - they were all soon going to be so impressed with my imminent eloquence. In fact, Glasgow might even sack their drummer Paul and give me the job because of it and how cool I was about to look! Awesome!

Vinnie Appice was Dio's drummer, previously playing with supergroups like Rainbow and Black Sabbath, and was the younger brother of Carmine Appice, himself also a world-famous drummer. I couldn't believe that I was just about to actually meet this real-life rock legend!

Just then, there was a flurry of excitement at the table as those who were facing the door all stood up as one and someone said "It's Jimmy!"

Jimmy Bain, Dio's bassist had arrived.

We all stood up and moved towards him, shaking his hand and saying things like 'Great gig, Jimmy!' and 'Well played, mate!' and other such compliments that were genuinely meant. Jimmy, red-eyed from what I took to be tiredness, thanked everyone in a sort of Scottish/American half-mumble, went to the bar, ordered a beer and said "Put it on my room," and then walked back out of the door and up to his room, never to be seen again that night.

We all looked around at each other, slightly deflated and a bit bemused by this, and someone made a discreet sign that it looked like beer wasn't the only substance that the bassist had been making use of that evening.

"So, Martin," Mick piped up, prodding everyone else back into their former party mood again, "What's the awesome statement you're going to say to Vinnie?"

"Well, I'm going to tell him 'I saw you the last time you played in Glasgow and you were brilliant then and I thought that tonight you played just as well as you did then, if not even better', and I've been memorising that over and over in my head."

"Bloody hell, man," Mick laughed, "Watch out he doesn't fall asleep before you finish the line!"

There was once again, some movement at the door. By this time, everyone was spread around the room, two or three sitting down and the rest standing up in various splintered groups.

It was Vinnie!

Vinnie Appice is here and he's heading straight for me! I am SO excited!

This is it - last chance to practise! Hi Vinnie, yes, I enjoyed your performance tonight. In fact, I heard you play the last time you were in Glasgow. You were brilliant then and I thought tonight you played just as well, if not better! (Smile and wait for the adulation from the Rock Legend).

By chance, I was standing next to the door and just happened to be 'First in Line' (a little Dio joke there), and Vinnie Appice, looking fit and just like the rock icon he was, walked straight up to me and thrust his hand out, which I eagerly shook.

"Hey, man," he drawled. "Did you enjoy the show?"

Then, inexplicably through a mixture of fear, awe, excitement and alcohol my brain did the cerebral equivalent of simultaneously urinating in its own trousers, shouting "TIMBER!" and falling over backwards, unconscious into a hedge.

"Hmmm… did I enjoy the show…?"

What the hell are you doing?! You're not meant to say that! Stick to the script, you imbecile! Tell him he played just as well, if not better!

"I've heard you play better."

Well done, you utter tit!

Vinnie didn't say a word and his expression didn't change one bit. His smile was still fixed as he turned to Steph on my left and extended his right hand.

"Hey, man. Did you enjoy the show?"

He said it in exactly the same tone as before.

Exactly the same.

"Oh, wow! You guys were AMAZING!" Steph gushed.

"Well thank you so much!" said Vinnie, and proceeded to have an actual conversation with Steph, and for some strange reason never spoke to me for the rest of the evening.

I did end up sitting for hours with the totally wonderful and humble Ronnie and his wife Wendy, who was also Dio's manager, and Vivian Campbell, Dio's outstanding lead guitarist and I really did have the most amazing time.

I'll definitely never forget it though, and not just because I got a "rock horns" salute from Ronnie James Dio all to myself as I left at 4am, that kept me floating all the way home that night.

I've often thought about writing to Vinnie via his management, to try to explain what actually happened that night, but I always end up with the sneaking suspicion that I probably remember it a lot more than he does.

Chapter Four

One Won't Kill You

Around the half way point of the first term of my third year, I found myself in a bit of a moral dilemma.

Well, maybe not so much a moral dilemma, but more a dilemma of principles, I suppose.

The way I dressed at that time more often than not had a distinctive semblance of heavy metal to it, and with usually a t-shirt and black biker jacket, complimented nicely by a pair of silver spandex trousers and white Adidas boxing boots I was the pinnacle of sartorial elegance, I thought. With long, loosely permed curls, and even though I looked less like Jon Bon Jovi and more like Deirdre Barlow, a stranger in the street could quite confidently wager that I was definitely a metal-head.

As the previous academic year had progressed, both Gibbo and Pam had increasingly been on at me to get my hair cut which I'd so far managed to successfully ignore. "And take that bloody earring out too," Gibbo frequently said. "You look like a poof."

Pam tended to be a bit more politically correct in her delivery, going for more of an explanatory and cajoling strategy. "Martin, all those permed curls would look right out of place on top of a set of tails, you know. I wouldn't book anyone who looked like that, so get rid of it and who knows, you'll probably start coming in with us," meaning the SNO.

This all just served to make me even more determined to not cave in to them.

What difference does short hair make? It won't make me play any better and only a few months ago I won the RSAMD Board of

Governor's Recital Prize for Percussion, so I know I'm not
completely rubbish at it, therefore it's purely someone else's
narrow-minded opinion of aesthetics. Anyway, if I did go and cut it
all off, there's no guarantee that I would be booked to play with the
SNO, as Pam does all the bookings for her section and she's just
used the word 'probably'.
  No, I will not get it cut and that's the end of it!
  Even so, no matter how much I resisted, the war of attrition over
what was perceived to be an unacceptable appearance for a
professional player with the country's national orchestra was slowly
being won by my teachers. I was aware of a couple of my peers
beginning to be booked by the SNO, and I had to eventually face a
decision - either transform my image against all my principles and
by doing so, start to work with the national orchestra that I'd been
training and studying for years to play with, or keep the status quo
and build resentment from both sides which would inevitably be a
disastrous move on my part and the highly probable end of any
possible career in orchestral playing before it had even started.
  Faced with what now appeared to be an obvious choice, I decided
to give up the fight and succumb to the barber's clippers and put my
red lightning bolt earring away in a drawer, and one week later, Pam
booked me for three concerts - a week's work - with the SNO.
  So, in January 1987, with mixed feelings of excitement and defeat,
and cold, bare ears I found myself in the Henry Wood Hall on
Claremont Street, home of the Scottish National Orchestra and my
first rehearsal for a week of playing bass drum in Ravel's 'Alborada
Del Grazioso', under the metronomic baton of the red-haired
conductor Christopher Seaman, or 'The Clockwork Orange' as he's
known by the players.
  Meeting everyone I'd only ever seen from a distance before, as
they'd been on stage and I was in the audience, was quite a head
spin, and to be still a student and surrounded by the top players in
the country was at the same time pretty daunting.
  One of the other players in our section that week was another
percussion student - a beautiful, smiley blonde girl called Gillian
McDonough who was Scottish but studying in London and a
fantastic player, especially on the tuned stuff. This week was her
first week with the SNO too.

It was great to have Gillian there, and we both propped each other up all week as it helped us both to know we weren't alone with our respective nervousness. It turned out to be a really enjoyable experience all round, which was also helped immensely by the fact that everyone made us newbies feel very welcome.

It was actually my third time playing with a professional orchestra, as I'd already popped my pro cherry in 1986, about one year previously with a couple of rehearsals and a one-off concert in Edinburgh with the Scottish Chamber Orchestra.

At the time, I knew that the men in orchestras wore tails but I didn't know that it was Evening Dress they wore at concerts or even that there were different types of dress tails at all.

I turned up to the SCO concert with what I found out later was a set of Morning tails, which I'd bought specially from a Glasgow shop that sold ex-hire clothes. Even with my Metal curls I still looked more like an undertaker than a musician and the SCO players were more than happy to point that out, much to their amusement.

A few weeks after the SCO, I got my first concert with the BBC SSO. It was a week playing 'Der Prince von Homburg' by Hans Werner Henze.

Apart from it being horrendously difficult to play, it was also notable for the fact that it was conducted by Fedor Glushchenko.

A Russian 'old school' conductor, the humourless Glushchenko would stop the rehearsal every two or three bars and usually tear a strip off someone for playing something that wasn't to his liking.

I must admit that, although the constant stopping was not altogether unappreciated by me as it meant I had more time to try and work out the immensely complex rhythms on my part, it did make me wonder if I'd made the right choice to be an orchestral player. Everyone was terrified for the entire week, wondering when it would be their turn to feel the wrath and vicious tongue of the man.

At one point, as he'd stopped the piece for the millionth time, he turned to the double bass section and asked them to play a passage on their own. He let them play for only two bars and raised his hand to silence them. The basses stopped and waited to hear what he thought was wrong with what they'd just played.

"*Contrabassi*, there is absolutely nothing I can do to improve that," he said in his thick Russian accent. "It is a conservatoire problem," he said with a look of contempt and a little dismissive flick of his raised hand, inferring that the whole of the BBC SSO bass section were not only unable to play that passage, but in his opinion also unable to play anything at all as they'd obviously wasted their collective time as music students, didn't have any talent whatsoever and shouldn't be anywhere near an instrument.

This, of course, only served to cement the animosity that the whole orchestra felt towards him, and to this day I've never met a nastier conductor than Glushchenko.

Anyway, as it turned out, I must have gotten away with my SNO week because at my next lesson Pam booked me for another week's work, this time 'Scheherazade' by Rimsky-Korsakov which would also be part of the orchestra's programme for their upcoming tour of Japan in October of that year (although I didn't know that yet) and this was closely followed by a few more bookings after that.

One of the pieces coming up was Prokofiev's epic score to the Russian movie 'Alexander Nevsky' and would involve not only a couple of concerts as part of the SNO's season but would also later be recorded for CD too - my first professional recording! Then she told me that, before the recording happened, it would also be part of the programme the SNO would be performing at the London Proms a few months later at the Royal Albert Hall - my first Prom!

I was well chuffed, and I'll always have a soft spot for both 'Scheherazade' and 'Nevsky'.

As the time went on and I was booked for more SNO work, I started to spend quite a lot of time with Alan 'Starky' Stark, their Sub-Principal (Number Two) Percussion.

I also started to spend quite a lot of money with him too, as our natural habitat very quickly became the pub.

Starky was from Chester-le-Street and spoke with a soft but fairly distinct Durham accent and didn't take too kindly to being labelled from Newcastle. He always not only looked older beyond his years but also had a maturity beyond them too. Or at least that's the impression I got as a player in my early-twenties, just starting out and trying not to make too much of an idiot of myself in front of the old pros.

I've always said that I learned more about the orchestral world from Starky in one night in the pub than I did from four years at Music

College, so by that criterion he is probably the person who has had the most influence and impact on me. I still stick meticulously by one of the first things he said to me and I usually mention it at every opportunity to younger players, whether they want me to or not as I have a good reason for doing so, involving an incident with the BBC SSO at the Proms in 1995, and I'll tell you all about that shortly.

"Rule number one: Don't draw attention to yourself or - more importantly - your section."

Yep, that seemed like solid advice.

In those early days, in the mid to late 1980s and gathering pace into the 1990s, the very prominent drinking culture involving the majority of orchestral players in the preceding decades was definitely waning.

In fact, wondering why it had been chucked out of the party, as it staggered up its own garden path at 2am, singing loudly and trying to fit its oversized key into its front door's shrinking lock before tripping over the door step, falling in and spending the night face down, with its feet still outside and its tongue stuck to the hall carpet, the notion of being drunk at work had become very unpopular indeed.

Whether it's on stage during concerts or even at the rehearsals leading up to it, it has continued in that direction, exponentially to the constantly skyrocketing standard of playing, both expected from and being produced by professional orchestral musicians today.

Now, I have to be clear about this.

When I say 'drinking', I'm not talking about a pint of lager or a glass of wine with lunch - something that an everyday office worker could maybe partake of with no discernible effect. I'm not even talking about the same office worker going out drinking with their mates on a Friday night and ending the evening with a nightclub, kebab and a fight.

I'm talking of a level way beyond that.

I'm talking about drinking to a plateau that would make Oliver Reed, Ernest Hemmingway and Elizabeth the Queen Mother all genuflect in deference to it.

The actual subject of drinking is a very emotive one in Orchestra-World, with 'So what's the cut-off limit then?' and 'It's impossible to police it' and 'I can't play without it' probably the most used phrases in any discussion on the subject.

There is a huge amount of tales that everyone has heard, of the preceding decades' worth of incidents of total mayhem through inebriation and quite often, alcoholism. Tales, both cringe-inducing and more often than not, hilarious, that usually serve as a dire warning to others with their moral normally being 'don't get so drunk and do something to the level that would put you in the unenviable position of there actually being a story about you.'

Even so, lunchtime drinks, post-rehearsal drinks, pre-concert drinks and post-concert drinks were normal for a lot of players on working days.

Sometime in the mid-to-late nineties - I can't remember exactly when, ironically - I made a rule for myself that I wouldn't drink before I played and I've stuck to it ever since with only a very few exceptions, none of which are in the slightest bit worthy of mention…I think.

There were a few reasons for doing this.

For a start, I really didn't like the feeling of not being in total control of my playing and decided that any mistakes that I made should be my own fault entirely and not because of alcohol, so even one drink was out of the question as I'd never be sure which one of us was at fault.

Another reason was that I could see and most definitely hear the colleagues who were on the Orchestra Drinking Team in each of the orchestras that I played with, many of whom were and still are very good friends, constantly draw unwanted attention to themselves and their respective sections from all corners of the stage, auditorium or pit, and it always reminded me of something that Pam said to me during a concert with the SNO one day, in the early days while I was still a student.

During the interval, as we were chatting in a backstage corridor just as a tail-coated player walked past us in the direction of the stage in a slanting, dressage style, carrying their violin and trailing whisky fumes, she said "There's plenty of time to get drunk after the concert - there's no need for it beforehand," and it's always stuck that I think she had a point.

There was also the fact that if I was the one who had paid a lot of my hard-earned money to take my wife, girlfriend or whoever to hear a concert by a supposedly top class professional orchestra and discovered that a few of them were allowed onto the stage inebriated, I'd be absolutely raging, to be blunt about it.

It's an inexcusable show of contempt for the audience, one's colleagues and not least, the music itself.

All of these reasons aside, the final straw and biggest catalyst that put the brakes on it for me was actually financial.

Drinking at every opportunity and constantly buying rounds is really expensive, and the people around me were not slow drinkers.

The worst times were after I joined the Scottish Ballet Orchestra in autumn 1989 and we were constantly off on tour around the UK.

Strangely enough though, they were also the best times for the very same reasons.

Our typical daily routine was approximately, but not confined to the following itinerary; some drinks at lunchtime before heading off to play the afternoon matinee, with another couple of drinks in the interval of the show. Then head to the pub as soon as it finished and keep at it until the evening show interrupted the merriment at 7.30pm, with a couple more in the interval again. Then, when the evening show finished, it was time to start 'proper' drinking and in whichever city we were in, we'd go to the pub until it shut and then find somewhere else that was open, usually a night club or casino or suchlike, after which we'd all head back to someone's hotel and make use of their all-night drinks via the night porter.

And we did that every day.

The real killer for me was the tours that we did of long, three-act ballets (usually Tchaikovsky ballets) with two intervals per show. Our 1995 tour of Swan Lake lasted for thirteen weeks and was comprised of seventy-two performances, each one of which had two intervals, and I came home after that tour with a lot less money than I had before it had started.

Mind you, that wasn't as bad as one of our hard-drinking woodwind players who, after a week in Hull - the eleventh week of that tour - arrived home for his one day there before heading away again the next day, only to find that his two young children didn't actually recognise him.

However, all that aside, I have to hold my hand up and admit to many occasions in the years before my self-imposed rule came into effect where I was definitely not a shining example of abstinence, so I'm certainly not going to judge anyone personally here, only the ethic, as that would be completely hypocritical. I will purely attempt to convey, in any situations that warrant it, the fact that alcohol is or was a factor.

A rather fine example of this, which barely springs to mind, is one particular Scottish Ballet performance of 'Who Cares?' in the spring of 1990, with music by Gershwin in which I was playing drum kit.

I do remember, however, that it was a lovely, sunny Friday and we were in our second week of the Glasgow part of the six-week tour, before taking it to Edinburgh, Hull and Newcastle.

As was usual for Fridays, there was only an evening performance that day and so I'd also managed to fit in a recording with the BBC SSO for that week. On the morning in question, the recording had finished at lunchtime and I had left the BBC Scotland building on Queen Margaret Drive and walked across the bridge to the BBC Club situated on Botanic Crescent, a highly desirable street and the place where a lot of us musicians spent most of our free time.

The Club was a place where BBC staff and their guests, other freelance members like me and associate members could go and relax. It was also a place that any of the big stars that were working at the BBC could go for a quiet drink without being harassed by the general public.

I had a pal who was there every day, and this particular day was no exception. Martin Black was a Glaswegian actor who'd appeared in a lot of television productions. He always used to talk about how he was big pals with Billy Connolly after they had both worked on the television production of 'Just Another Saturday', a play about the Orange walk culture in Glasgow and part of the BBC's 'Play For Today' series in 1975.

As I entered the Club at around 1pm, I bumped into Martin who was heading past me and just leaving. "Martin!" I said as I stopped him. "Where are you going? It's your round!"

"Not to worry, dear fellow," he replied in his actor's RP voice that he often used for implied comic effect, before switching into a hybrid one of RP and Glasgow Ned.

"One is only heading doon Byres Road and shall return presently. At aboot hauf two."

"Ah, I'll be away by then," I said, disappointed that I'd miss him. "I've got a show tonight, playing kit, so I can't really drink anyway. Even one drink and my body doesn't do what it's meant it to."

"Ah well, until next time then, good sir!" he exclaimed, and bowed with a flourish before giving me the V's with a grin and exiting stage left.

I walked into the small but busy bar area and ordered a fresh orange and soda.

"A *what*?!" was the incredulous retort from Danny, the manager of the Club. "Are you ill or something?"

"Ha ha, very funny," I said sarcastically. "I'm playing kit tonight and it doesn't mix well with booze."

"Do you mean it doesn't mix well for you, or the audience?" he joked.

"Both! I'm serious, Danny! I literally can't play at all. All my arms and legs all go at the same time and there's nothing I can do about it."

Danny laughed and poured me a fresh orange and soda, and I stood at the bar on my own, sipping it slowly and trying to convince myself that I really didn't want a beer.

Around two o'clock, the Club started to thin out and the lunchtime mob began to leave, and head back to work over the road. There were now only about four or five people left, scattered about the area, including myself still standing on my own at the bar, having now made two fresh oranges last almost an hour.

I had my back turned to shield my eyes from the low springtime sun that was streaming in through the three massive bay windows in the lounge, so I never saw the next person that came into the bar but was only aware of their presence when they spoke.

"Hi, is Martin Black around?"

There was no-one else at the bar, and Danny had disappeared into the cellar, so I presumed they must be talking to me. I turned around to see Billy Connolly standing beside me, and I have to confess I did a little '*Ooooh, it's Billy Connolly!*' in my head.

"He's gone down Byres Road but he should be back here any minute now," I said, feeling proud of myself that I hadn't dissolved into a giggling mess in front of the man whose VHS videos I'd bought – every one of them - and had watched continuously for years.

"OK, I'll just hang on here for him."

"No worries. Would you like a drink?" I asked, fully aware that he'd been famously teetotal for years.

"Yeah, I'll have a coca cola, thanks." I noticed he didn't say "Coke" like the rest of us mere mortals would, and even made "coca cola" sound amusing.

Danny appeared and I ordered the drinks.

"A coke and another fresh orange and soda please, Danny."

"Another one?! Jesus, Martin, just have a pint. One isn't gonna kill you!"

I thought about it for a second.

Well......it's two o'clock and if I have one now I can make it last until Martin Black gets back here to take over, plus it'll all have worn off by 7.30pm tonight so I'm sure I'll be fine. Anyway, I don't want to leave Billy Connolly standing here all on his own....

Who am I kidding?!I'm here on my own with Billy Connolly! I'm not going anywhere until I need to leave at 7pm!

"Ok, Danny," I said, happy that it was all someone else's idea and nothing whatsoever to do with me or freewill or anything. "I'll just have one."

And that's the last thing I remember.

I have a few flashes of going to the bar many, many times and also of sitting in a group, so I think more people must have joined us, with the comedian holding court and possibly using us as guinea pigs for some new material, but the next proper thing I'm aware of is being awakened by the light streaming in through the thin curtains on my bedroom window as I slowly and painfully opened my eyes.

I looked at the digital radio alarm on my bedside table and it read 13:15.

13:15?!

It's Saturday afternoon!

I've got a matinee in forty-five minutes!

I somehow managed to shower, dress and get to the Theatre Royal, plonking down on my drum stool less than ten seconds before the orchestra tuned.

52

With red-flushed face, all sweaty, shaky and still very confused, and definitely still not sober, I detected some un-subtle chuckling from the players behind me. I turned around to see the trombones and tuba all smiling at me. I nodded a silent 'hello' in their direction and one of them laconically returned the greeting with "Afternoon. Heh heh!" and a wink.

Oh no, what did I do last night?

I did discretely ask some people later, and I was definitely there and playing, and by some bizarre stroke of luck I didn't get sacked or even called into the management office or summoned to the conductor's room.

But to this day I've got absolutely no recollection of playing the show which, conversely, is why it's so memorable.

I also want to make clear that with regards to drinking, I'm only talking about the orchestral side of things and professional orchestral players.

Jazz is completely different.

Another regular in the BBC Club was Dave McClelland, an amazing jazz trumpeter with the BBC Scottish Radio Orchestra, the corporation's broadcasting big band in Scotland.

I had - once again - finished a SSO rehearsal day just before lunchtime and had arrived at the Club around 12:30pm, just as Dave was leaving.

"I'm just off down Byres road to get my eyes tested," he said "It's that time again!"

A short time later Dave returned and we drank steadily until almost 5pm, when he slowly and very drunkenly said "Right, I'm jusht off down Byresh Road to get my eyesh teshted."

"No, Dave," I said "You did that earlier, remember?"

"Of course I remember, but that was for my normal seeing specs," he slurred. "This one is for my playing specs."

The Scottish Ballet Orchestra's Principal Double Bass, Rick Standley, joined the SBO at the same time as I did.

He told me of a gig he went to at the famous Ronnie Scott's jazz club in London, where Ronnie Scott himself was playing that night, with his quartet. As the second half of the gig was about to commence, only three members of the quartet took to the stage and Ronnie approached the microphone.

"Ladies and gentlemen, is there a bass player in the house?" he announced to the now slightly worried audience. "Unfortunately, ours has been taken unexpectedly drunk."

The biggest problem about mixing alcohol and playing is that ninety-nine per cent of the time, it breaks Starky's First Rule of Drinking and Playing, which I proudly take credit for clumsily naming it back in the day, even though I'm totally aware that it's been around for much longer and not confined to just the music world.

The inescapable fact is that by its inherent nature and no matter how hard one tries to hide it, drinking to excess will always draw unwanted attention through many of its manifestations.

Mainly it achieves this by causing the player to play either out of tune, un-rhythmically and dynamically impaired or usually all three along with a multitude of other unmusical afflictions, while at the same time being totally oblivious to both it and to the rest of his or her colleagues cringing in embarrassment.

However, out of everyone I know, there are two people who are exceptions to this, and both of them are cellists.

We were all standing around in our tails during the interval of a concert somewhere on a tour of Austria and Germany in the mid 1990's, drinking our half-time coffees and I was chatting to one of the cellists, who'd been given leave from his own orchestra specially for this tour. He had just played the most beautiful solo in the first half even though I knew him to be completely wasted, and I genuinely wanted to know how he did it.

"That was just stunning, mate." I said. "But how can you play like that when you're so pissed?"

"Because I practice when I'm pissed," was the slurred but honest reply.

Fair enough.

A friend of mine, himself an ex-alcoholic and currently teetotal for over twenty years, was one of the principal players in both the Royal

Philharmonic Orchestra and the London Symphony Orchestra during the 1960's and 1970's and is still brutally honest about the level of drinking at that time.

"We were all on a bottle of whisky each before lunch," he told me. "Pretty good going when that includes a three-hour rehearsal, 10am-1pm so the only free time you've got is from when you arrive at the venue until the rehearsal starts, and a twenty-minute break around 11.30am. It probably helped that most of us were already well gone when we arrived at ten, though."

"Did no-one say anything?" I asked him. "Surely every single person in the band wasn't hammered?"

"No, not everyone was but most of us were, including the management so there was no point in complaining to them about it. Anyway, it was different in those days. If you had a problem with someone you'd go up to them and tell them and that's how we sorted things out, not all this running to the management and complaining about colleagues that goes on these days. And do you know how that managed to work?"

I genuinely had no idea how an orchestra of seventy to eighty people, the vast majority of whom had been drinking to a level that would get a normal person thrown out of a pub and an ambulance called, could coherently and objectively settle any disputes between themselves without the aid of Henry Kissinger and the Red Cross.

"Nope, sorry," I replied. "I've got no idea."

"No women."

He was serious.

"What do you mean, 'no women'?"

"The band was all blokes, so we sorted out our problems like blokes. It was in the days before women started playing in major orchestras."

"I couldn't imagine an orchestra without women," I said. "I'd hate that - it would be so boring! I'm glad they're here."

"Don't get me wrong, I am too. It's just that it was a different time back then. A different era."

To illustrate that for a moment, my best friend Anne ('cello, BBC SSO) studied and worked in Austria for fifteen years before arriving in Glasgow, via Italy. She told me that a lot of the Austrian orchestras, the few remaining ones to deny women full-time positions, eventually did advertise posts in the early 1990's. After the list of audition requirements, it said "Disabled people and women may apply for this position if they are at an equivalent standard to men."

Nice.

Anyway, back to my friend again, and I asked him if the general public, or 'punters' as they're referred to by the players, ever got an inkling of what went on or if they were totally unaware that the world-renowned orchestra they were listening to was actually ninety percent proof?

"It's hard to tell at concerts if anyone noticed, as we just played the concert - and played it well, I might add - and left, and I don't remember hearing anyone in the audience commenting or anything like that."

I get the impression that what he was really trying to say was "It was hard to tell because we were all drunk."

This all leads nicely into the next chapter and an incident so surreal that I'll quite honestly never forget it.

Chapter Five

No Sign of Tony

Oh, it was not so tragic and Heaven did not fall
But how much at the time I hated being there at all
Jacques Brel, 'Next'

Tuesday 8th August 1995 is a date that will live, maybe not in infamy as, thanks to the Imperial Japanese Attack on Pearl Harbour and Roosevelt's subsequent speech to Congress, that word is the sole property of Sunday 7th December 1941.

It will, though, be indelibly printed in my memory and definitely burned into quite a few others. Namely, the memories of those who were either in the audience of the BBC SSO's Prom at the Royal Albert Hall that night, or those in the proximity of that orchestra's percussion section.

And for two reasons.

Firstly, it was one of those extremely rare occasions where a Prom concert was brought to an unscheduled, premature finish by outside forces and secondly, it was my colleague Tony.

Tony was a very well-liked, well-spoken Englishman who at one point had been Principal Percussion with the City of Birmingham Symphony Orchestra and had left there to take up the same position with the London Philharmonic Orchestra.

Apart from being an outstanding percussionist, an incredible musician and all-round decent bloke, Tony was also a highly talented pianist.

As I've mentioned already, everyone had to play piano as a second study at college, and I was no exception. For the RSAMD's entrance audition, I played an Associated Board Grade Five piece, which was the minimum required standard. This was, in fact the only piano piece I could play, as Mr H our High School music teacher, taught both Doug and I to play it specifically for our respective auditions. "That should get you in to the Academy," he said. "After that, you're on your own."

After three years of intensive study at the Academy and three years of even more intensive piano practice and lessons with Jean Hutcheson, a professional pianist and altogether lovely lady, for my final exam I played a Grade Four piece.

So technically, my piano playing actually got worse.

Tony however, wasn't in my lowly league - he was an excellent pianist. He was also always very pleasant and polite to everyone and had some great stories that kept people entertained at length.

Unfortunately, though, and to be diplomatic about it, Tony always preferred to err on the side of bacchanalia, and most of that good stuff tended to disappear when he was under the influence and he had lost all sense of inhibition and social protocol.

He had by this time, managed to get himself 'rubbed' (removed from the list of extra players used by orchestras) by almost every orchestra in mainland Britain, purely through alcohol and it had got to the stage where Heather, Principal Percussion at the BBC SSO was the only one who would book Tony for any work, as both his playing and personality had very sadly become extremely unpredictable.

As percussionists, we have to both set up and pack away our section and all the percussion instruments needed for each programme, so we're always the first to arrive at rehearsals and the last to leave after concerts, sometime hours after the rest of the orchestra have gone.

On this particularly sunny Tuesday in August, the rehearsal was at 10am-1pm with a break until the evening concert at 7.30pm, and because there were two contemporary pieces in the second half which required a ton of percussion, we arrived early at the RAH at 8.30am.

Specifically, Dave, Heather and I turned up, but there was no sign of Tony.

"I'm sure he'll turn up soon," I said half-heartedly to the other two, although from our experiences of the previous few years, we all knew that in reality Tony might not turn up at all and if he did, there was every chance he wouldn't be much use to anyone.

I think now is a good time to mention the programme for that evening, along with a little technical info;

Fantasy Overture 'Romeo and Juliet' – Tchaikovsky
(Piano move)
Rhapsody on a Theme of Paganini – Rachmaninov
INTERVAL
Orchestral Theatre I: Xun – Tan Dun
Orchestral Theatre II: Re – Tan Dun
Symphony No 9 in E flat major – Shostakovich

Tan Dun would conduct his own two pieces, and the rest would be conducted by Jerzy Maksymiuk, the SSO's Polish Conductor Laureate and also their ex-Principal conductor from 1983-1993.

Our not inconsiderable set up for the concert comprised a 'normal' percussion section (bass drum, cymbals, snare drum, etc., referred to by us as 'usual percussion' or abbreviated to 'UP') for the entire first half and also the final piece in the second half, plus four individual multi-percussion set-ups for the two Tan Dun pieces, one set-up for each of the four players.

The three of us started emptying what seemed like dozens of flight cases full of percussion gear and finished the set up - including all of Tony's gear - with about fifteen minutes to spare, so Dave and I headed downstairs to the Artist's Bar for a quick coffee before the rehearsal started.

As we walked in, the first person we saw was Tony, sitting at one of the small wooden tables with a fresh orange juice in front of him.

"Tony mate, where were you? We were worried," said Dave. "Heather's going mental because you didn't show," he added.

"Ah, you worry too much, Dave," Tony replied with a little smile and seemed oblivious to the fact that we'd just set up all his gear for him. "I'll smooth it all out when I get up there."

"Well, best of luck with that, Tony," I said with a dubious look. "We're having a coffee do you want anything?"

"I'll have a fresh orange juice, thanks Mart. In a large glass, please." Tony was one of the few people that called me 'Mart', which I actually quite liked.

I brought two coffees and a large glass, half-filled with fresh orange over to the table and sat down with Tony and Dave.

Tony picked up the glass of orange juice he already had and downed it in one. Suddenly, he stood up and said "Back in a minute, chaps," and quickly disappeared out of the Artist's Bar door, taking his new orange juice with him.

Dave and I looked at each other and said nothing. We were both fairly sure Tony had gone to his not-so-secret stash of vodka in his bag that he'd left in the gent's band room.

Sure enough, two minutes later, Tony reappeared and sat back down at the table, placing his 'orange juice', which was now miraculously full to the brim, in front of him.

Needless to say, due to his magic orange juice, the rehearsal didn't go particularly well for Tony - and therefore by proxy - the whole percussion section.

In particular, towards the end of the first Tan Dun piece, there is a long and extremely quiet passage played by the upper strings which lasts a good couple of minutes until it's suddenly interrupted by the four percussionists simultaneously playing a loud *forte-piano* roll on woodblocks.

It's difficult at the best of times to get four players to play exactly together, so that the listener only hears one entry and not two, three or four, and even more so when it's played on an instrument like a woodblock which sounds immediately when struck. At the rehearsals in Glasgow in the preceding days, this particular percussion entry was the main focal object of Tan Dun's obsessiveness for minute detail.

Although it would be six years before he would win the Oscar for Best Original Score for 'Crouching Tiger, Hidden Dragon', even at that time Tan Dun wouldn't let anyone get away with anything if it wasn't perfect. He knew exactly what he wanted and would make you play it over and over again until it was exactly right.

"No, percussion!" he'd shout. "Too quiet! I want it louder!" which was pretty unusual because he'd normally be shouting "Too loud, percussion! I want it quieter!" at us.

This time though, it was mostly "You're not together! Do it again!...... No, still not together - again!...... No - again!......" for what seemed like an eternity. It was all the more frustrating when we knew that there was one of us who was drunk, and it was really no wonder that it wasn't together.

I liked Tan Dun. He wasn't nasty like a lot of conductors are, and off the podium he's quite a funny person. He just wanted to get everything exactly right.

Back in the RAH, we finished the three-hour rehearsal with the two Tan Dun pieces and a huge sigh of relief, and I turned to the others and said, "Right, I'm off - see you tonight. I'll probably get back here for about half past six."

"Yeah, that sounds good" said Dave. "See you at reception in the hotel at six and we can walk up together." And with that we all left and went our separate ways to find something to occupy ourselves for the next five and a half hours of free time before we were due back at the hall again.

Or six and a half hours of free time before the concert started.

You can get a lot done in London in six and a half hours.

You could, on average, run the London marathon approximately one and a half times.

Or you could get the Eurostar train from St Pancras to Paris; back again to London; watch a full Millwall-Chelsea match and still have fifteen minutes spare to have your stitches done at A and E after the game.

Or, at a rate of £1 for one minute, apparently, you could spend three hundred and ninety pounds peering through a letterbox in a Soho peep show.

As we were about to discover, you could also do a lot of drinking in six and a half hours.

I met Dave at reception as we'd arranged and started the fifteen-minute walk from the hotel on Gloucester Road to the Albert Hall, with only one subject of conversation.

"We'll probably be ok tonight," I said. I was a bit more hopeful about this than Dave was. "He's had enough vodka and orange this morning to warrant a good sleep this afternoon, so he'll have slept it all off. Shouldn't be too bad, I reckon."

Dave looked sceptical at that. "Well, Marty, we'll soon find out."

We arrived at the stage door and after being buzzed through by security I said to Dave "I'm just going to check my gear and get changed while the band room's quiet," so I headed onto the stage, checked all my stuff was exactly where I'd left it five and a half hours ago, and made my way to the gent's band room.

I typed in the four-digit door code we'd all been given earlier and walked in, just as Dave appeared behind me at speed, and I held the door open for him.

"I just bumped into Heather" he said, slightly out of breath and with a hint of urgency. "Tony's drunk."

"No....... how badly?"

"Absolutely plastered! He's in the Artist's Bar now, slumped over a table - literally. At least he's already changed into his white jacket though."

"Bloody hell, Dave. So, it's not looking good for the Tan Dun, then?"

"Marty, it's not looking good for the whole concert, I'm sorry to say. Heather is going apeshit again."

We quickly changed into our black trousers, white shirts, white jackets and black bow ties, and headed to the scene of carnage in the artist's bar.

There was no sign of Tony.

"He was here less than ten minutes ago at that table and I couldn't wake him!" said a puzzled Dave, indicating a cleared table with nothing to suggest that it had recently been used.

Just then, Tony entered through the door, again with a large glass of what looked like fresh orange juice in his hand, full to the brim but expertly carried and not a drop was spilled as he slowly and carefully sat down at the table next to which we were standing.

We sat down too.

"Good evening, chaps" said Tony in a surprisingly coherent delivery, and then cancelled it out by continuing with what sounded like "Howsh wshhh faaaaaaaahhnn, tehh?" in authentic drunken gibberish.

62

"How are you feeling, Tony?" I said deliberately slower and slightly louder than normal as though I was speaking to a deaf, elderly relative in a nursing home.

There was no answer, as he'd closed his eyes and fallen asleep.

"*Shit*...." said Dave quietly. "We're on in five minutes! What are we going to do? We can't let management see him like this..."

I had an idea forming. "It's just you and Heather in the overture, then there's a piano move, right?" Dave nodded. "Ok, take his glass and get rid of it on your way out, but first bring back a coffee, and if he asks where the vodka's gone, I'll say he finished it earlier. The Tchaikovsky is twenty minutes long and the piano move is at least five minutes, so from now we've got just over half an hour before he has to play. It's better than nothing. I'll sit with him and try and get the coffee down him."

So, a black coffee appeared and Dave left to join the rest of the orchestra for the overture, putting Tony's glass on the bar counter on his way past, just as I managed to get Tony to open his eyes. "Tony! Mate! Wakey wakey! Drink your coffee, mate, we're on soon!"

He immediately began to jump into life and looked at the cup of black coffee in front of him. "Where's my orange gone?"

I noticed that the professional drinker in him said only "orange", omitting anything incriminatory.

"You finished that earlier," I lied.

Out of the corner of my eye, I could see his drink still sitting on the bar where Dave had left it in full view. The one young girl who was the sole bar person was out from behind the bar, collecting glasses and cleaning the tables and I just hoped that Tony wouldn't spot it too. "They've just started the overture, Tony so we'll need to head upstairs in a minute," I said to distract him. "Drink your coffee."

To my surprise he picked it up and took a massive gulp. "Oooh, that's hot!" he said, and then finished the whole thing with a second and final gulp.

As soon as he put his cup back down I said "Right, let's go" and stood up, ready to help him to his feet but he seemed to manage that fine on his own, giving me a little glimmer of hope that everything would be alright after all.

The overture had only been going for about three minutes or so, but I'd no idea how long it would take to get Tony up the backstage flight of about twenty stairs that went from the main backstage corridor which ran around almost the whole circumference of the Albert Hall and would take us up to the door that both we and the audience used, situated just behind the percussion section.

We were the only section that entered this way. Everyone else came onto the stage via two sets of double doors that opened from two mini corridors that connected the backstage corridor to either side of the stage, known as the right and left 'Bull Runs'. There weren't any steps on stage up to our level, so the percussionists entered from the back and walked down about six or seven elongated steps - about twelve to fifteen feet long in total - then through a little gap in the handrail separating the stage and audience and voila, we were in our section.

We weren't there yet, though. We were just leaving the bar area, slowly but fairly steadily and I was leading Tony and constantly talking to him to try to keep his attention. I turned around to make sure he was still following me and still standing upright, and to my horror I saw him spot and pick up the full glass of vodka and orange from the bar as he walked past. By this point, with the many top-ups of Smirnoff's finest, it was now almost completely straight vodka with a small pipette's worth of orange.

"Ah, there it is!" he said with an expression akin to seeing an old friend after a long absence.

"Tony, don't drink that, mate!" I said "Put it back down and we can get it at the interval." But it was futile. He didn't drink it, but he didn't put it down either and tightly kept hold of it as we passed the right Bull Run and prepared for the tricky ascension of the stairs.

For what should have taken six or seven seconds, we made it up the stairs fairly swiftly, all things considered, in about a minute or two and moved into a little vestibule area in between two sets of double doors. One set separated us from the Front of House corridor that the audience used and the other set, along with a heavy, red velvet curtain was the only thing now between us and the audience.

It's probably safe to say that, at that moment, I was more than a bit concerned.

In this little area where we now were, there were four small steps leading to a raised, carpeted walkway which ran parallel to the outer corridor and led to the production room which housed a large BBC mixing desk and a lot of the top management and producers, and also the room where the BBC radio presenter sat for every concert, all of them broadcast live. Tony, gingerly and in slow motion sat down on these little steps, still holding his drink, and let his head droop forward again and I frantically hoped no-one would choose that moment to walk past.

I couldn't shout or even speak loudly, as the audience and BBC Radio microphones were immediately on the other side of the door, so I kept talking to Tony in a loud whisper, trying my best to keep him awake and had another idea.

There were still about ten minutes to go before the overture was finished, but I guessed that if he thought we were about to go on, then I could somehow distract him and I'd be able to get his drink away from him and place it out the door, in the corridor and out of harm's way, and we'd have a few more minutes of respite.

To be honest, I hadn't really ironed out the finer points of this great idea, but it was at least an idea and anyway, it was the only idea I had.

I bent down to Tony, now slumped forward, asleep again and even though there were still ten minutes to go, I loudly whispered "Tony! We're on in two minutes!" and prepared myself to quickly take his drink from him.

Now, if you've ever tried to take a drink away from a drunk, you'll be aware of how dangerous and downright impossible it actually is, and there's probably more chance of being able to grab a viper by its throat while you're facing it and using your weaker hand.

On hearing that we were on, Tony opened his eyes, straightened up and saw me move my hand towards his drink whereupon, with the speed of Hermes, he quickly put it to his lips and drank the whole large glass of almost straight vodka in one elongated go. He put the empty glass down beside himself, stood up and immediately began retching. He wasn't sick but was at that point where it could go either way.

We stood there for the next ten minutes, Tony supporting himself with his right arm on my left shoulder, head down and retching, and listening to me trying to speak calmly to him and hoping with every fibre in my body that he wouldn't throw up, and not just because he was inches away and facing towards me.

If that did happen, very shortly the doors would open for the interval and the audience would stream out and have to negotiate an Olympic-sized pool of orange vomit, in the middle of which would be a white-jacketed musician curled up in the foetal position, and I would be long gone.

Tony held his nerve and his insides, and the retching gradually died away until eventually we heard the Tchaikovsky finish and the audience applaud.

"Are you ready?" I asked him and he nodded. "Ok, I'll go first in case I need to catch you. Just go slowly and hold onto the handrail. It's the piano move now, so we've got time."

I opened one of the double doors, pulled aside the curtain and we slowly walked into the packed auditorium - and were hit immediately by the room's notoriously unpleasant stifling heat.

Onstage, Dave and Heather were both looking back at us, horrified, as they watched us slowly walk the short distance down to the section, with me in front walking backwards, ready to catch Tony who was holding the handrail with both hands and slowly moving sideways down the stairs like Marcel Marceau, but with an actual handrail. We got to the gap in the rail and I held Tony and guided him in, past the other two and along to the bass drum at the end of the section, sat him down and took my place next to him, at the cymbals.

I was sweating.

I looked at the other two as they looked back in open-mouthed silence and disbelief and I said to them, with absolutely no conviction "We're fine. Everything's fine."

The piano move involved uprooting almost the whole string section, with the cellos, violas and second violins all leaving the stage, and the first violins standing up and moving to the back of their section and out of the way. The crew then move all the vacated chairs and music stands, wheel in the soloist's grand piano and put it in its pre-designated position at the front of the stage, move all the stands and chairs back again and everyone then retakes their places, ready to start the concerto.

As the crew were at the point of initially removing the chairs and stands, and the first violins were milling around their area, there was a general murmur from the audience as they quietly chatted while waiting for the Rachmaninov to start.

That's when Tony, who'd been dozing peacefully for the past couple of minutes since sitting down, suddenly stood and picked up a bass drum beater.

The three of us watched on with unfolding horror as he slowly drew the stick in his right hand back to a distance way behind his head and aimed his left hand at the centre of the large forty-two-inch diameter bass drum, as though he were about to try his luck on a 'Hit This Thing as Hard as You Can' stall at a funfair. He held himself like a statue in that position for about four or five seconds, and then to everyone's great relief eventually slowly lowered his arm.

I turned to the other two, both of them now ashen-faced and wide-eyed and was about to say something like "That was close," when Tony quickly, and in one fluid movement raised his hand again, only this time he followed it through with the hardest strike I've ever witnessed by any player on any instrument.

It was like a Howitzer firing.

The Royal Albert Hall has a capacity of 5,272 seats, and every single one was occupied for tonight's Prom, along with a jam-packed standing-only prom area containing another few hundred people. The general murmur that had gently been going on suddenly became a split second of total shocked silence as everyone in the auditorium got the fright of their lives, before it was then quickly replaced by a loud muttering of irritated punters.

Totally unaware of it all, Tony sat down again and said to himself "Yes, that sounds fine", obviously happy with the drum's tone.

I looked at Dave who was now sitting with his head in one hand and I heard Heather say from the level behind us "Oh no, no, no. We can't have that!" but completely powerless to do anything about it.

Tony was still oblivious to it all though, and as the strings filed back onto the stage to start the piano concerto, it shortly became clear to us that he had only just got started.

For this Prom, everyone had new parts (sheet music) for the Rachmaninov. Years of use and constant pencil markings being made and erased had left the original orchestral parts in a sorry state and so the brand new, easy to read parts were welcomed with approval by the players.

With one small exception, that is - the percussion parts.

Originally, we had individual parts for each instrument, meaning the bass drum had its own part, as did the cymbals, likewise the snare drum, etc., but the new parts were now in score form, meaning everyone's part was identical, with all the instruments now on their own line on the same page, like a conductor's score, and before the first rehearsal we had to mark each of our own respective lines so that it was easier to read.

The audience, now a little bit calmer applauded and Maksymiuk walked onstage, following Stephen Hough, the highly acclaimed world-class pianist and soloist for the Rachmaninov.

The players in the percussion section are all involved during the introduction of the piece, playing various quiet, unobtrusive single-note interjections on all of their instruments, and as it started we were all as focussed as we could be on getting our parts right. That didn't last long though, as Tony, obviously confused by the new score parts, played every note that came along, on the bass drum, whether the note happened to be on the cymbal line, snare drum line or whatever. Every single note.

It sounded like an Orange band had arrived.

Not long into the piece there are four bars of quiet, off-beat cymbals, not too tricky but it can sound a bit ropey if it's not perfect. I stood up, played the short passage and luckily it went fine, and I sat back down and concentrated on my next upcoming entry.

Now, in orchestras, if someone plays something that warrants a 'well done' or 'bravo' from their colleagues sitting near them, they quite often get a little 'shuffle' from those colleagues. If the colleague is playing, they will lightly and discretely, as though scratching their sole, slide one of their feet back and forwards a couple of times so as not to make a sound that would be heard by the audience, but would be heard by the player who'd just impressed them. If they are not playing at that point, they instead might - once again lightly and discretely - rub their hand back and forth against their knee a couple of times, which will nearly always be seen by the intended recipient who will discretely acknowledge it and everyone carries on with the job in hand.

Lightly and discretely, so as not to draw the audience's attention to surplus or extraneous noise or movement that would distract them from their otherwise enjoyment of the music.

As I sat down after playing that little cymbal passage, Tony very kindly gave me a light and discrete hand-against-knee shuffle, to which I discretely acknowledged by turning slightly towards him and giving him a small nod - *'thanks'*.

Tony obviously didn't spot my acknowledgement, so he leaned forward and lightly but a little less discretely rubbed the stick tray (called a "trap" tray) in front of him, on which sat four pairs of heavy bass drum beaters, or eight single heavy sticks depending on how you count them. I quickly looked at him and gave one big, obvious nod of my head - *'THANKS'*, and returned my gaze to the front and my concentration to Rachmaninov.

Tony obviously, once again, didn't spot my acknowledgement, so he leaned forward again and rubbed the trap tray with enough vigour to cause six of the sticks to fall off and onto the wooden floor of the Albert Hall stage with a prolonged loud clatter, leaving two odd ones rolling about on the tray, one eventually coming to rest precariously half-on, half-off like the final scene of 'The Italian Job'.

There wasn't much I could really do with that, so I steadfastly stared forward and tried my best to totally ignore the chaos beside me.

Tony obviously didn't spot that after two acknowledgements I was now deliberately trying to ignore him, so he swivelled his stool ninety degrees to his right, now facing me, and side-on and in profile to the audience, pumped his fists with both thumbs up, back and forwards less than an inch from the side of my face.

I couldn't believe this was happening.

I could feel over five thousand pairs of eyes looking in our direction for all the wrong reasons and I just wanted the stage to swallow me up.

I sat absolutely still, not even glancing in Tony's direction and hoping his arms would soon tire and he'd stop pumping his thumbs at me.

After about ten seconds that felt like ten hours, Tony stopped and wordlessly swivelled back round and faced the audience once again.

My heart was beating furiously.

I'd never experienced anything like this in a concert before anywhere, never mind at the Albert Hall AND it was being broadcast live not only UK-wide as normal, but for one night only it was going out as a special Europe-wide broadcast!

Holy shit! This is insane! At least there's a bit of bass drum coming up now, so that'll take his attention away from me.

And so....

Four bars to go before Tony's bass drum entry....

Three bars to go....

Two bars.... Tony leaned over and picked up one of the remaining sticks from the trap tray.

Bar before the bass drum entry.... Tony leaned over and put the stick back down, swivelled his stool round to face me again, grabbed my left arm and started violently shaking it and shouting "Well done, Mart! Well done!" as the mad shaking caused another stick to roll off the trap tray and join its pals on the Albert Hall floor with another wood-on-wood clatter.

I had my arms crossed and Tony wouldn't let go.

He kept shaking and shaking and shouting "Well done!" until I forcibly tore my arm out of his vice-like grip.

"Ah, suit yourself," he slurred, swivelled back to face the front, lowered his head and fell asleep.

Tony slept, motionless for the next five or ten minutes, his bass drum part going past, unplayed, until we reached the most beautiful part of the piece for most people - the famous Eighteenth Variation. As it headed to the magnificent, emotional climax, with the whole orchestra playing their hearts out and not a dry eye in the auditorium, out of the corner of my eye I saw movement on my left.

The Kraken had awakened.

He lifted his head and as the music reached its orgasmic zenith, he shouted "This is my favourite bit!" and sang/shouted along with the tune "Dah dah da da DAAAAHHH!" and loudly whacked the dead centre of the drum with his empty hand.

Even the soloist looked up at us from the front of the stage with an open-mouthed expression which unmistakeably said "What in the name of Rachmaninov's ghost was THAT?!"

As the piece continued, Tony went back to sleep again.

Well, he tried to sleep but it soon became apparent that he wasn't comfortable. He then tried to alleviate the discomfort by crossing his legs. This didn't happen though, as his legs were definitely not working and by the looks of it they'd been the first part of Tony's body to ignore brain signals, ahead of everything else. This wasn't going to stop the determined drummer, however and so he decided to do it manually. He reached down with his right hand, grabbed the top of his right sock and pulled with all his might.

Unfortunately, his leg turned out to be pretty heavy, so that didn't work, and Tony gave it up as a bad idea and again went back to sleep.

He had, however, forgotten to let go of his very stretchy sock, the top of which he was now still holding against his right cheek, elbow sticking out at a ninety-degree angle like a sculpture of a plastered archer aiming his invisible bow at the loose pile of bass drum beaters rolling about on the ground, and the other end of his sock still full of right foot and still on the floor.

And that's how he stayed, feeling no pain, until the piece finished.

INTERVAL!

There was nothing that anyone could say - we were literally speechless.

Tony disappeared for the duration of the interval, and returned for the start of the second half, the last to come on stage and just before the conductor, Tan Dun himself.

We (the four percussionists) had our multi-percussion set-ups on two levels of the stage. Tony was on my right with Heather on the upper level directly behind me, and Dave to the right of her and behind Tony.

To put it tactfully, 'Orchestral Theatre I: Xun' was an unmitigated disaster.

We had score parts again, and Dave told me later that he looked down at one point, as Tony was standing, arms outstretched, holding a pair of cymbals in position for about a minute, ready to crash them together, and saw that he wasn't even on the right page. When we actually reached the infamous woodblock entry, I thought Tan Dun was going to walk through the orchestra and punch one of us, as Tony played his entry, not only a nanosecond before the rest of us, but three whole bars, about fifteen seconds' worth. At least he'd got back onto the right page by then.

As the piece finished and the conductor stood every section up individually during the applause except us, there was an unexpected announcement over the PA system in the auditorium.

"Ladies and gentlemen, unfortunately we have to cancel the rest of tonight's concert. A public generator in South Kensington which provides all the power for the Hall has blown itself up. Please leave the Hall by the nearest exit in an orderly manner." I got the impression that the person doing the announcing didn't really have very good 'people' skills and this was confirmed when they added "But don't hang about as we're now using our back-up generators and they'll only work for three more minutes, after which the hall will be plunged into total darkness, and I mean pitch black. Thank you."

And so, we all left, still in our concert dress and walked back to the hotel and got exceedingly drunk for the rest of the evening, with no sign of Tony.

In all seriousness, it was really sad to see a once outstanding player now hopelessly lost in such self-destruction, and so much so that the BBC SSO management had no option but to remove Tony from their list after that night. He was already booked for the following week; a concert at the Edinburgh Festival, and they grudgingly allowed him to do it but that's a story for another time, and that was the last any of us have seen of Tony.

I later heard from one of his ex-students who is now a full-time percussionist with English National Opera that Tony had an open-air performance of 'Carmina Burana' with the RTE Symphony Orchestra in Dublin, the last orchestra left that would take him on and, sadly, that concert too was an ordeal for those around him.

As the performance was about to start, the Principal Percussionist looked around his section and saw no sign of Tony. With a sigh of disappointment, he said to the player next to him "Looks like he hasn't made it out of the beer tent," and the piece started.

O Fortuna!
velut luna
statu variabilis

Then the chorus continued with

semper crescis
aut decrescis;
vita detestabilis.

Well, most of the chorus sang that.
There was one voice that didn't.
From the front row of the chorus a well-spoken, English accent was loudly singing, albeit slurred, something completely different. Tony wasn't still in the beer tent after all but had somehow managed to get in amongst the tenors and was happily singing along and pointing at the conductor on every syllable, like a bouncing ball on a karaoke lyric screen.

toss-pot wan-ker
toss-pot wan-ker
you fu-cking toss-pot wan-kerrrr

Classic.

Playing bass guitar with my best friend who started it all, **Dougie Vipond**, in concert with school rock band, "**Spectrum**", 1984. Doug's "rebellious teen" t-shirt didn't go down too well with the teaching staff, I remember.

Ragamuffin supporting an up-and-coming **Deacon Blue** at the RSAMD's Stevenson Hall, 1986. *(l-r)* **Matthew Pearce**, "**Diamond**" **Dave Rousen**, Martin Willis, **Jimmy Murrison**.

My dog-eared, 2ndYear **RSAMD** matriculation card. "Looking less like Jon Bon Jovi and more like Dierdre Barlow…."

Graduation day, 1987. At Glasgow University with proud parents, **Margaret** and **Martin**.

Suntory Hall, Tokyo - SNO, October 1987. *(l-r)*, Starky, Elspeth, Gibbo, Ian, Pam. (I took the photo).

Istanbul's Atatürk Cultural Center, a prestigious venue on a tour of **Greece and Turkey,** SNO, 1990.

The only professional photo I've ever had taken. BBC SSO Principal Conductor, **Osmo Vänskä** was having a press photo shoot on the stage of **Glasgow's City Halls** before a concert and I hijacked his photographer, 1997.

With **Anne**, at a colleague's wedding, 2006.

Overlooking beautiful **Bergen, Norway,** RSNO, 2004 and sporting what appears to be a rather fine mullet. I don't remember ever having that hairstyle, so it must have been the breeze or something, honestly.

I made Gibbo laugh in **Stockholm, Sweden,** RSNO, 2004. I'm not saying how, so you'll just have to use your imagination.

Chapter Six

Meet the Ultras

As the middle of May 2004 approached, the Spanish journalist and television news anchor Letizia Ortiz was growing excited. She was about to marry Prince Felipe of Spain in Madrid and become a real life fairy-tale princess, the lucky girl. At the same time, over 1,400 miles away in Glasgow, some of the ladies and one bloke, musicians of the BBC SSO were excited about the wedding too. The orchestra was about to embark on a one-week tour of Spain and would be in San Sebastian on the 22nd of May - the same day as the royal wedding.

We would be playing in Oviedo, the capital city of Asturias, then moving on to Madrid for two concerts before travelling just over 300km north east to Zaragoza for one concert, and from there back up again to the very north of the country and San Sebastian in the Basque region, on the morning of the 22nd for the final concert.

Before we set off though, we had still to play a concert in Glasgow of the programme we'd be touring, as is normal procedure. This gives the orchestra a dry run at the programme which avoids the possible situation of playing it in concert for the first time in an unfamiliar hall, while more than likely over-tired from travelling and would therefore make the orchestra, to use a technical term "sound like shit."

Well, it's normal procedure for most orchestras, that is, as long as they're not the RSNO being conducted by their Chief Conductor on a one-off concert in Baden-Baden in Germany on 26th January 2008.

This conductor, apart from being referred to by the players as either 'Mick Hucknall' or 'Angry Kid', due to his unruly mop of crazy, tight red curls which gave him a similar appearance to both the lead singer of Simply Red and Channel Four's foul-mouthed clay animation, was notorious mainly for his ability to talk through the most part of any rehearsal.

During the rehearsals for the Baden-Baden concert, we were all immensely impressed and suicidally bored in equal measures by his capacity for long-winded explanations of how he perceived the music and how it should manifest itself.

So much so, that some players surreptitiously videoed him in full flow, to prove to others who thought the stories about him too far-fetched, before their respective phones ran out of battery power or memory, so prolonged were the dismal and bizarre monologues to the orchestra.

At these rehearsals in this particular week, he was in a singularly monumental rambling mode and because he had talked for so long, by the time the concert in Baden-Baden arrived, we hadn't actually played the last few pages of Strauss's 'Don Juan' and so the whole orchestra were literally sight-reading it during the concert.

Don Juan is played fairly regularly but is a difficult piece, so even the seasoned professionals have to keep on top of it and put a lot of practice hours into it before the first rehearsal. Some passages are so tricky that excerpts from the piece are always on the audition lists for nearly every orchestral instrument, and not to at least have a run-through in rehearsal is a pretty major oversight by any conductor.

Sight-reading Richard Strauss to a German audience!

I know that there are much worse things in the world, but it's the artistic equivalent of Claude Monet having an exhibition of his work, inviting only art critics and trying to distract them by saying "Sorry folks, this one's almost finished. If you just look at them Haystacks I done earlier, hanging on that wall over there, I'm just gonna finish off colouring in these Lilies" and then hang it up when he thinks no-one is looking.

Everyone was totally focussed, and with extra-heightened senses and a huge amount of luck, the piece went well. I was particularly impressed by how well the RSNO strings coped, especially the violins, whose last page of that piece is almost completely black with notes and they nailed every single one.

To top it all, the encore was Bizet's 'Farandole', a staple encore for orchestras the world over and features a *tambourin provençal* (field drum) which starts solo and plays a continuous repeated four-note pattern with an accent on the first note of every four.

During rehearsals, as Simon, now the RSNO's Principal Percussion, played it exactly as written and exactly like it had been played by every drummer since it was first performed in 1872, the conductor stopped the orchestra and said "No, Simon. There should be no accent there at all. It must sound like a dance, like this," and then proceeded to sing the melody in a strange mixture of styles, gesturing with his hand a flat, even line. He kept singing for almost thirty seconds (try it - it's a long time) and even when Simon said loudly "Yes, I get it - no accent," he still continued.

When we got to the actual encore in the concert and Simon started to play as he'd been directed to by the great maestro, with no accents anywhere to be heard and every note perfectly identical to the previous one, the conductor looked over at him with a face full of anger and shouted – yes, shouted – across the orchestra "ACCENT!... ACCENT...! ACCENT!" on the first of every four, emphasising each one with a pointed finger at Simon.

The drummer was absolutely livid, and when the concert finished and the applause had died away, he raced off the stage and headed straight for the maestro's dressing room, ready to give him what's usually termed "a right good bollocking", only to find a queue of irate Principals already waiting in line outside the room to do exactly the same thing for a long list of other reasons.

Back in Glasgow in 2004 though, the BBC SSO were much better prepared for their Spanish tour under the baton of Ilan Volkov and were now sitting on the stage of the City Halls, playing to a capacity audience.

Dave, my mate and partner in crime since RSAMD days sadly wouldn't be on this tour because of an upcoming operation. Decades of bad cymbal technique had taken its toll on his left shoulder.

I'm kidding, of course. It was his right shoulder.

Anyway, the final piece in the concert was the Suite from Stravinsky's ballet music 'The Firebird', another staple of the concert platform. I recently spoke to Ilan regarding this Spanish tour and he described that piece to me as "a good piece for touring because it sounds harder to play than it actually is", which made me smile because it's true and I hadn't realised it before.

Volkov, an Israeli of Ukrainian and German descent and a tightly-wound ball of perpetual energy was the BBC SSO's principal conductor from 2003-2009, and at 26 years old was the youngest principal conductor ever to be appointed to a BBC orchestra.

With metaphorical ears like a bat and able to pick out one wrong note from seventy musicians playing seventy different parts simultaneously, he is one of the very few conductors for whom I have the utmost respect, and even in spite of his fiery temperament, and the fact he says "timpanis" giving the word a double-plural (timpani is already the plural of timpano), I like him a lot and always look forward to the weeks he's on.

So, talking of princesses earlier, in the years after he'd written the complete fifty-minute ballet, Stravinsky produced three different suites from it. These shorter suites, arranged in 1911, 1919 and 1945 all have the same core numbers with other numbers added to the preceding suite, and the 1919 version being the most popularly played. In each suite, the Princesses' Rondo is always followed with an immediate *segue* into the Infernal Dance of Kastchei, and I'm sure Stravinsky did that deliberately for his own amusement, as will soon become apparent.

The City Halls concert had sold out quickly, so they opened up the choir stalls behind the orchestra to the public, and abruptly sold all those seats too.

One of the bonuses of being the bass drum player in 'The Firebird' comes just as the lightly-flowing, beautiful Rondo finishes with a slow *rallentando* into a very quiet sustained chord played by only a few players. Suddenly, every player on stage then plays one very short, *triple forte sforzando* note as loud as possible, to start the Infernal Dance and the bass drum player, who's usually standing or at least sitting higher than everyone else, gets to see the vast majority of the audience who are not expecting it, jump out of their seats with a real fright, as though someone had crept up behind them and burst a blown-up paper bag in their ear.

At the Glasgow concert this happened as it usually did, with one new extra addition to the brief moment of light relief for myself on bass drum.

Having played that opening *triple forte* note, the piece continued
with the French horns' quiet, menacing melody and I counted the
next few bars before the next *triple forte* note, but before it arrived,
and around eight or nine seconds into the movement, a little
Glaswegian voice from the choir stalls directly behind me said in a
very loud whisper, *"Jeeeeeesus CHRIST! I've shat myself!* "I turned
my head ever so slightly round and saw a small middle-aged man
who'd slid almost off his seat, clutching his chest with his right hand
and with a wide-eyed look of relief that he was still alive.

I'm ashamed to say that I made quite a loud snorting sound as I
tried unsuccessfully to stifle a laugh and played the rest of the
movement from memory as I couldn't see anything because of the
tears streaming down my face.

A few days later, we were in warm and sunny Oviedo, where we
found a cider bar after the concert and experienced the famous
traditional cider-pouring from the waiters. Theatrically holding a
glass in one hand as low as possible and with the other, lifting a full
wine-bottle sized bottle of cider as high above their head as they
could and pouring it, all without looking was highly impressive
indeed.

I was enjoying Spain. It was my first time in that country, with a
week on holiday in Majorca ten years previously, being the closest
I'd got to it at that point. I tried to soak in as much of the Spanish
culture as I could in the short time we were there, and by the time we
reached Madrid the next day, I was fluent enough in Spanish to get
me out of any emergency.

"Una porción de patatas fritas y una cerveza, por favor," which I
believe will alleviate most perilous situations.

The orchestra were all up early that day, and we left Oviedo on
three coaches for a journey of five hours or so to Madrid. There was
the inevitable complaining from a large portion of the players, the
main subject being the rather long time that everyone had to endure
sitting on a coach while the orchestra manager had booked himself
and the conductor onto a direct flight at a fraction of the orchestra's
travel time.

This particular journey was always going to be tight, as we had a
rehearsal as soon as we arrived in Madrid, and that couldn't go past

its finishing time either because there was a concert by another orchestra immediately after our rehearsal.

All was going to plan and we arrived at the impressive Auditorio Nacional de Mùsica with just enough time for us percussionists to set our gear up and listen to Ilan Volkov having a meltdown.

We hadn't realised it but one of the coaches had got lost and so a third of the orchestra were missing. There was no point in rehearsing anything with that number of absentees, so everyone tried to stay out of sight and earshot of Ilan who was absolutely fuming and shouting at everyone, players and management alike.

My favourite was, to a hapless violinist; "What do you mean you're going to the toilet?! Get back on stage!"

The concert that evening passed without incident and after it had finished we all trudged back onto the coaches.

We eventually debussed outside what would be our home for the next two nights, the beautifully named Hotel Colon, which predictably induced a few puerile sniggers mainly from the brass and percussion sections.

There was just enough time to queue up for our room keys, dump our bags and head back down to a small bar that someone had spotted not far from the hotel. We stayed there for a bit longer than we normally would, as we'd been told by the management that tomorrow's rehearsal time had been put back. We'd played the programme a few times now and so only a short seating call was needed. This meant we now had a few unexpected hours free the next afternoon, and so our mini late-night *fiesta* cranked up a couple of notches.

After breakfast the next morning, I met up with five or six others and we decided to go for a walk into the centre of Madrid and explore for a bit. As we left the hotel, we were passed by Eddie Gallagher, the orchestra's stage manager also on his way out from the hotel.

"Morning, Eddie," I said. "We're going into town for a wander, want to come along?"

Eddie, a lifelong Celtic supporter, loved football in general and had booked himself on a tour of Real Madrid's stadium, the impressive Santiago Bernabéu.

"Thanks, mate," he replied, "but I'm off to the Bernabéu! I've booked a tour for eleven o'clock, so I'll catch you later."

Hotel Colon wasn't that far from the city centre, and quite close to both the famous Las Ventas Bullring and Retiro Park, a vast green space full of sculptures, monuments, galleries and even a lake, and is bang in the centre of the city.

Our little group walked around until lunchtime, taking in the sights of beautiful Madrid and eventually found a small restaurant with enough free space for us all to sit outside for lunch.

On a tall stand in the outside seating area, the restaurant had a large flat-screen television on which it was showing bull-fighting live from the nearby Las Ventas ring. This is the only time I've ever seen a bull-fight and I have to say it was not particularly enjoyable. As I watched the faces of the crowd in the bullring I got the distinct and indelible impression that it was just a replacement for the spectacle of a public execution, in the days when families would take the kids for a day out to see someone being disembowelled over their sandwiches.

Not literally *over* their sandwiches, but you know what I mean.

Before long it was time to head back to the hotel and freshen up before getting the coach back to the Auditorio Nacional de Mùsica again for the second and final concert in Madrid.

A modern looking, late 1980s building, the Auditorio Nacional de Mùsica housed a few performing venues, with the main Symphonic Hall being the largest at just over 2,300-seat capacity. It was a grand, bright auditorium, with plenty of backstage space which went down well with everyone.

The hall's choir stall section was slightly lower than the one in Glasgow's City Halls, with the top of the wooden barrier at the front of the section now at my shoulder-height as opposed to just above my head-height, like it was back in Glasgow, and although the concert wasn't completely sold out, they had still opened the choir stalls for sale to those punters who prefer to sit behind the orchestra for whatever reasons. Sometimes it's to follow our percussion parts, which all the players and especially Dave, don't like one bit. There's nothing more off-putting and distracting than being aware of someone looking over your shoulder and following your part during a concert.

'The Firebird' made another appearance to finish the concert, and when the Infernal Dance started, I once again got a brilliant view of the almost-full auditorium jump in shock at its opening note and smiled a little smile to myself.

Then the most amazing thing happened.

From behind me, in the choir stalls, I heard a little, shaking Spanish voice loudly whisper what I made out to be "HAY- SOOZ!" and after a few seconds it dawned on me that it was Spanish for "JESUS!"

It was at exactly the same moment in the music as the poor unsuspecting punter in Glasgow gave his holy utterance and I thought then and there that music is indeed an international language that speaks to everyone, regardless of where they're from.

Then I realised with a sudden, deep profundity, it can also make people of all nationalities, creeds and colours lose control of their bodily functions in equal measure.

After the concert, we all went back to the same bar that we'd been in the previous night, and when the place closed at midnight, headed back to the hotel. Many of us were not quite sated though, and so were on the lookout for more refreshments in another bar that we hoped to find on the way there.

We made it all the way back to Hotel Colon with no luck in finding one and as most of the players headed off to bed, I bumped into two of the crew coming down the stairs from the main entrance and onto the pavement outside. It was stage manager Eddie and assistant stage manager Eldon Byrne, one of the nicest and hardest working guys I've ever had the pleasure to meet. They had just arrived at the hotel, having finished their work a couple of hours later than the orchestra due to clearing the stage after us and loading the instrument truck ready for its journey to Zaragoza the next day.

"Hey guys, where are you off to?" I asked them. "Do you know somewhere that's open?"

"We're going to the bar that everyone was in last night" said Eldon.

"We've just come from there," I said and gave them the bad news. "It's shut, I'm afraid."

"There must be something still open," said the ever-optimistic Eldon. "It's Spain! I'm going to ask at reception if they know of anywhere."

"Well, I'm coming with you," I said and followed the pair of them into the hotel lobby and up to the counter at reception.

A clean shaven, well-groomed receptionist in his mid-twenties sat behind the counter, dressed smartly in a white shirt and grey striped hotel uniform tie which was set off nicely by an immaculate black blazer, and greeted us with a welcoming smile as we approached him.

"Good evening, gentlemen" he said in perfect English with only a small nuance of a Spanish accent. "How can I help you?"

His name was Sebastián, according to the name badge he wore on the left lapel of his blazer.

"Hi, mate" said Eddie. "Do you know of anywhere that's open at this time for a beer? We've just finished work."

The receptionist thought for a couple of seconds.

"Hmmm.... Not much open at this time, I'm afraid. There are a couple of places, but I wouldn't send you there. Too dangerous for non-locals."

The three of us gave a little collective disappointed sigh.

"Ah well," I said. "We tried."

We turned and started to walk towards the lifts and up to our respective rooms.

"Wait!" said Sebastián, his face lighting up as he just remembered something. "There's a place not far from here at all. It's called 'Bar Eclipse' on the Calle del Dr. Esquerdo – about three minutes' walk from here."

"Really? Excellent!" said Eddie.

"Yes, go out of the hotel, turn right and you'll be on the main street called Calle del Dr. Esquerdo ("Doctor Esquerdo Street" in English). Turn left and it's a couple of blocks, about four hundred metres down the hill on the right-hand side."

"Thanks, Sebastián!" I said. "That's brilliant!"

"You're welcome!" he said with a large grin and he seemed genuinely happy to have helped us.

We followed his directions and sure enough, after three or four minutes we spotted a squat little building with a white awning-covered entrance and the word 'Eclipse' next to a round green and white neon sign for Heineken beer.

The only cars we could see were the ones parked along the length of both sides of the street, and so the three of us crossed the deserted, eight-lane-wide, tree-lined Calle del Dr. Esquerdo and walked the short length of the building's mirrored, white greenhouse-like exterior, underneath the awning and up six or seven stairs, opened the door and went inside.

We were immediately met by two bouncers, massive guys dressed all in black, one of whom held open another door for us and silently nodded a 'Buenas noches' as we walked into the main bar itself.

The room was hot and deceptively large, in a rectangular shape with the bar along one and a half sides of it. Spanish pop music was blasting from the speakers in each of the four corners and although it was dimly lit, I could clearly see a couple of guys playing pool at a table in the middle of the room, and around twenty other people, all blokes, most of them in their early to late twenties, already in the place and my first impression was that Sebastián had sent us to a gay bar.

I really didn't care though. *As long as they've got beer!*

Eddie went straight up to the fairly busy bar and ordered three beers. The barman drew three little lines on a beer mat and handed it to him, a tab to be paid at the end of the night as is the custom on the continent, and we moved around to a section of the bar away from everyone else. Eddie and Eldon both sat on tall wooden bar stools facing each other and surveying the room and I stood facing both of them, with my back to the room. I told them about Jesus and The Firebird to their great amusement, and Eddie excitedly told us about his trip to the Bernabéu that morning.

Pretty soon our drinks were empty and I picked up our beer-mat tab and went back to the bar, inadvertently choosing a busy period for the barman, and there were four or five people ahead of me waiting to be served.

I was standing there patiently amongst the small throng when a guy on my left turned to me and smiled.

"Hi. Are you having a good evening?" he asked, once again in perfect English. He appeared to be in his early thirties, with a short, well-groomed beard and a pleasant and friendly demeanour, and as I will usually talk to anyone, especially after a couple of drinks, I smiled back.

"Yes, great thanks. Your English is excellent" I said. "But how did you know I wasn't Spanish?"

"Oh, we heard you talking earlier. Are you English?"

"No, we're Scottish," I told him, and then explained that we were working with an orchestra and had just finished playing at their national auditorium.

"Cool! I used to play the 'cello when I was at school and I love music!"

We chatted at the bar for a bit and I found out his name was Max, he goes to orchestral concerts, supports Atlético Madrid and his daughter was only two weeks younger than my son. He was indeed a pleasant bloke and we hit it off nicely, and he even insisted that I was served before him at the bar.

After I was served, I said "Thanks Max, see you later," and I took the drinks back to Eddie and Eldon, whereupon I told them about the local I'd just met at the bar.

"Well I'm glad one of them is nice," said Eddie.

"What do you mean?"

"While you were at the bar, we were getting eyeballed by a couple of the guys at that big table in the corner. Look, but don't make it obvious."

I took a couple of sips from my beer, and as I had my back to the room once again, I casually turned to briefly face the room and turned back to my pals again.

"I can't see anything, mate. You're probably just imagining it."

"No," Eldon chipped in. "We were definitely getting the evil eye by two or three of them. I think they're all together, too - every single one of them in the bar. They're up to something."

I didn't believe that at all. "No, I'm sure it's fine," I said confidently.

Max, the guy I had just spoken to at the bar definitely didn't seem the type who was out for trouble and I told that to the other two and thought no more of it.

We started chatting again and after five or six minutes I realised that I was the only one doing all the talking and the other two were furtively but constantly looking over my shoulders at the rest of the bar.

Suddenly there was a loud smack from the pool table and the unmistakeable sound of a pool ball being potted with force followed by a shout of triumph from one of the guys playing.

At that point, I had the first nagging suspicion that Eldon might be right, as the pool guy's shout seemed to be a bit over the top and even though it was behind me, I felt it was aimed in our direction.

The next second, I heard someone approach us from behind and I turned to see one of the guys who'd been playing pool, now standing in between me and Eldon and still holding his pool cue, even though the game had just obviously finished. He wasn't brandishing it like a weapon but was still definitely holding it in a prominent position where he knew we could see it.

"You English?" he asked with a heavy Spanish accent. He had drooping eyelids as though he was either drunk or high, and because he seemed to be moving around fine I presumed it was the latter.

"No, Scottish," we said.

"Not English?"

"No, not English. We're from Scotland." This seemed to confuse him a little, and I've found it's not an uncommon occurrence abroad to be then asked 'Where's that, then?'

Two other guys from the other side of the room had now come over and joined the one with the pool cue, and I could see the rest of the guys in the room all starting to take a real interest in us now.

Out of nowhere, one of the blokes who'd just come over said with a growl, "In Spain, we KILL the bull!" and emphasised 'kill' with a stabbing motion with his right hand, and immediately repeated it. "We KILL the bull!"

I have been in some dodgy situations over the years and found myself in places where I probably shouldn't have been, and I've often had to take some delicate care with strangers whom I've just met, but I've always somehow managed to diffuse anything before it got out of hand and always woken up the next day unscathed.

This was completely different, and I had a real bad feeling about it now.

The three guys standing with us had now been joined by a fourth who I noticed had moved around the back of Eldon and now stood a few feet behind him.

This isn't looking good. How the hell do we get out of this? There's no way the three of us stand any chance against this lot....

Suddenly Max appeared and spoke in Spanish to the pool cue bloke. I heard the words "Escocés.... No Inglés!... Vamos, vamos!" interspersed in the middle of it all and he started to usher the four of them away and back to the pool table area, all the while arguing back and forth between themselves.

One of the black-clad bouncers came through the door and stood there, eyeing up everyone including us three.

Eddie slowly raised himself from the bar stool. "Right, I'm going to pay the tab now in case we need to leave in a hurry." And he went over to the bar and was back again a minute later, our tab paid.

The atmosphere was now tangibly menacing and we were still hearing the odd "We kill the bull!" randomly shouted at us from across the room and now from more than one voice.

I could see Max and another guy, both of whom appeared to be the two eldest of the Spaniards, walking around and talking and gesturing, sometimes shouting at and arguing with the rest of them, and the three of us all got the distinct impression that they were some sort of leaders in the group.

Just then, I felt a tap on my shoulder and turned around, genuinely expecting to meet something coming towards me with force and at speed, and instead I saw the original bloke who'd had the pool cue standing there with no cue or any weapon at all.

"Put your hand out. A present for you," he said, as he moved his hand to give me something.

Automatically, like a sheep, I opened my palm and he put one little sweet on it. A small, red conical jelly about a centimetre high and coated in sugar. A peace offering maybe, but at the same time I didn't trust him and I wasn't too keen on putting it anywhere near my mouth.

Immediately, Max appeared again, grabbed the sweet from my still open palm and said "Don't eat that!" He gave it back to Pool Cue Guy and again ushered him away from us, as they both had another heated argument while they moved back towards the main group.

Every one of them were now really agitated and arguing with Max and the other leader, and at one point we heard an almost pleading voice from one of them who said, in English "Why can't we do it? They are right here!" We were left in no doubt of its sinister meaning and definitely knew that we were meant to hear it.

That was it, we were leaving.

Unfortunately, though, we would have to walk through the whole mass of them to reach the door, and even though there was a bouncer there, I really didn't give us much of a chance of reaching it in one piece.

And anyway, the three of us all had the distinct impression that that wouldn't be allowed to happen.

Then, as if things couldn't get any worse, the bouncer disappeared back out of the door and we were left all alone with what was rapidly becoming a baying mob, held only in check by Max and his mate.

"*No…seriously? Where's he gone?!*" I quietly whispered.

Eldon gave me a sideways look and simply said quietly "Goodnight Vienna…"

As they were all arguing amongst themselves, shouting and wildly gesticulating, from out of nowhere, the bouncer who'd just left us suddenly appeared right beside us and said "You three, go now!"

He quickly led us through an open doorway in the wall, exactly where we were sitting. We hadn't even noticed it before, as the room beyond was in darkness. We followed him into the small, unlit room which turned out to be a dining area with a few tables and a little recess which housed another door, above which hung a fire exit sign.

The bouncer had chosen his moment to rescue us perfectly, and as we quickly walked towards the exit he said "You are lucky tonight." He nodded in the direction of the receding sound of arguing and said "Ultras."

The Atlético Madrid Ultras were infamous around the world as one of the most brutal organisations of football casuals, who amongst other traits fostered an abiding and fierce hatred of anything Real Madrid and had a membership of hundreds.

He pushed open the fire door and said "Pronto! Pronto!"

The three of us rushed out the door and into a back lane, and I said "Gracias seňor!" as I sprinted past him into the darkness, and he quickly closed the door behind us.

We turned to the right and in a few steps, we were back on the Calle del Dr. Esquerdo. We ran uphill on the long, straight boulevard pavement, all the time looking behind in the direction of Bar Eclipse for pursuers and thankfully seeing none. We kept running until we were almost at our street and we could see the top of Hotel Colon, proudly announcing its sanctuary in big white neon letters.

We were far enough away now and slowed to a walk. I off ripped my t-shirt, the adrenaline release taking over and we all let out loud, primal shouts of relief.

Right at that moment, from down the hill we saw the Eclipse spill out about twenty screaming, furious Atlético Madrid Ultras. They poured out onto the street and began frantically searching everywhere for us, and we watched them even checking underneath all of the parked cars on each side of the road, their frustration building and very obvious to us.

I sincerely believe that Max was looking after us purely because of the conversation I'd had with him earlier, when we discovered a few tenuous common bonds between us. Either way, if it hadn't been for his efforts I honestly think the night would have ended totally and catastrophically different.

Safe now in touching distance of the hotel and probably too far away for them even to hear, we bravely shouted various insults down the street at the Ultras and I put my t-shirt back on as we entered the lobby.

Sebastián was still at the front desk and so we went up to him and told him what had happened.

"It all seemed to come out of nowhere," said Eddie. "We were sitting on our own, not bothering anyone."

"Ah, but they are Ultras," Sebastián said. "They heard you all talking about the Bernabéu, home of the enemy."

We all were a bit confused by that statement.

"Wait a minute," said Eldon "How do you know they heard us talking about the Bernabéu?"

Sebastián smiled at us and lifted his hand to his blazer's left lapel and turned it over.

Pinned on the underside of the lapel was a small round red, white and blue Atlético Madrid badge. He gave us a little wink, put his lapel back and, still smiling said "Anything else I can do for you gentlemen?"

He was an Ultra too!

He'd sent us there deliberately.

We were speechless.

We all looked at each other in stunned silence, turned and walked away, which was without a doubt, the wisest action to take.

After all, Sebastián did know which rooms we were in, plus he also had the keys to them.

The three of us all went straight to my room and between us we drank the entire mini-bar. The next day I got a massive bill for it before we got on the coach to Zaragoza, but I didn't really care.

I was just happy to still be alive and able to pay it.

Chapter Seven

Short Rant in a Fast Machine

Touring abroad with an orchestra is usually viewed by the players in one of two ways. Three if you count the near-death experience of Spain but we won't, as that's extremely rare, thankfully.

The first way to look at it is that it's a fantastic opportunity to see parts of the world that one wouldn't normally visit, while at the same time experiencing different cultures and discovering how different audiences react to your efforts on stage. And all the while getting paid for it!

The other way that many musicians view foreign tours is that it's 'one big long bloody queue' where you don't have to think for yourself and just follow the person in front of you, with always at least one person doing sheep impressions throughout the tour.

Yes, it's true that from the moment you arrive at your departure airport, there's a queue to check in. Then, because there are usually seventy to eighty musicians adding to the no doubt already busy airport, there's a longer than normal queue for the coffee shop/bar. Then a queue to board the plane. Then one at the other end to check everyone into the first hotel of the tour and queues every day after that at each subsequent hotel to do the same. There are more queues at each venue too, whether it's at stage door security, the canteen, the one-person-at-a-time backstage toilets or whatever. Then you do it all again in reverse for the return trip.

But it's not exactly a life-changing, mental illness-inducing trauma though.

It's a slightly annoying occupational hazard, more in the vein of trying to get to sleep at night, with a solitary mosquito sharing your hotel bedroom. However, some of the moaning and complaints that go on would be utterly hilarious if they weren't so seriously meant.

I very much subscribe to the first view of touring abroad, and if I didn't still enjoy it, I definitely would not still be doing it.

I feel extremely lucky to be in the privileged position of being able to act like a total dickhead and complain, if I so wished, that my free Caipirinha, poured by a barman in a five-star hotel in Rio de Janeiro, who'll soon be going home to his shack in one of the gang-controlled, drug-ridden, murderous favelas, only has two wedges of lime and that clarinettist's one has got three in his. It's bloody ridiculous!

On tour, a lot of players - myself included - usually have small bets on who hears the first "it's ridiculous!" moan from someone.

The main contender for the winner of the Golden Snivelling Whine, an award I've just invented, is a classic from an orchestral tour of India in April, 2014.

Spouted by a poor disgruntled musician (on a full-time contract), it contains a heady mixture of pettiness, selfishness, bad grammar, grand delusion and a hint of the attitude that eventually got Britain kicked out of that stunningly beautiful country.

As we sat on a luxury coach from our very posh hotel on our way to play a concert at the Siri Fort in New Delhi, halfway through the fourteen-day tour during which we had - unusually - quite a bit of free time to ourselves, we drove past miles and miles of poverty.

Many people were sleeping by the roadside and I even saw families living under a motorway flyover which was horrendously noisy and constantly busy with traffic discharging all manner of black, polluting smoke from a multitude of exhausts.

As we drove a bit further, we passed a Jaguar car showroom. The three-story high, glass fronted building full of luxury cars was closed for the day's business and the doorway in the wide entrance to it was now crammed full of makeshift bedding and plastic bags, the only worldly possessions of an unnamed family who'd managed to claim this bit of prime real estate, at least for one night.

To me, the dichotomy of this image was simply staggering.

That was when a whining voice piped up with "It's SO hot on this coach! Is the air conditioning broken or something? Why haven't the management done something about it?! Even them out there (*the people sleeping in the gutter*) are out in the fresh air and we're stuck on this fucking coach! AND I was up at seven o'clock this morning because of those dodgy canapés we were served at the British High Commissioner's reception for us last night! It's RIDICULOUS!"

Ladies and gentlemen, we have a winner!

This attitude isn't too far removed from the one presented by a few players - and I must stress that it is only a very few - who display the rather unattractive trait of taking their respective employers for all they can get, for self-gain.

Abusing the system seems to be a bit of a hobby for the repugnant small minority who wouldn't think twice about, amongst many other things, going off 'sick' or 'injured' and providing a genuine doctor's note or sick line, so therefore still being paid. If one is genuinely ill, that in itself is a normal and acceptable practice obviously, but they then often give the game away by posting photos on social media of themselves playing on tour either at home or abroad with some other professional organisation (and also being paid by that unwitting organisation), all the while purporting to be too ill to go to work. They're smart, though. They know that their company is powerless to do anything because of the doctor's note and would be accused of harassment if they did query it.

It is only a few of the players who engage in this despicable behaviour, thankfully and no matter how accomplished a musician they are, I personally have nothing but utter contempt for them.

As it turns out, I'm not the only one either.

A few years ago, I was chatting with a player who had been appointed as a full-time member of one of the orchestras and had now been in the post for about a year. This musician told me that within their first week of joining, one of the long-serving members introduced themself and said "Welcome to the orchestra," which the new player rightly thought was a nice gesture.

The long-serving player then, straight away, said "I'll give you one piece of advice. As soon as you're back at work from any time off like summer or Christmas holidays, put a sick line in to say that you were ill during it and you'll get another couple of weeks off, fully paid. I do it all the time and it's great!"

The new person's response to me was "I immediately didn't like them."

I said "Everybody knows that particular player does that. They're also the same person who mysteriously goes off 'sick' every time their favourite football team is playing at home, dropping their colleagues right in it from a great height at the last minute, with absolutely no shame."

As a sixteen-year-old, I had a summer job as an auxiliary nurse at Erskine Hospital, as it was then known. It's original official name was The Princess Louise Scottish Hospital for Limbless Sailors and Soldiers, (later adapted to "Disabled Ex-Servicemen", to which "and Women" was subsequently added), and nowadays is known simply as "Erskine".

My mum worked there as the Personal Secretary to the Matron and had talked to me many times about the place, the patients and the staff who worked there and ultimately inspired me to apply for the summer job.

It opened in 1916 to care for the enormous amount of wounded arriving home from the battlefields of the First World War, as it quickly became apparent that there weren't anywhere near enough places or provision in the country to be able to cope with such vast numbers.

Almost every patient was there for the long-term, and by the time I started in summer 1982, there were patients of all ages, each with their own unique disability. Age-wise, they ranged from Michael, shell-shocked as a seventeen-year-old soldier in 1916 at the Battle of the Somme and was admitted in 1917, the year after the hospital opened and now at eighty-three years old and had never left the hospital grounds in all those years, to the contemporary young soldiers. Andrew, a nineteen-year-old (only three years older than me!) had been recently wounded in Belfast and was now permanently disabled but keeping himself busy by working in the hospital's workshop.

The job entailed mainly constant interaction with the patients, and we basically did almost everything that the trained nurses did, with the exception of giving out drugs or medicine. Talking to them and hearing their stories of what they all went through when they were my age really put a lot into perspective, and that particular outlook has stayed with me ever since.

I spent a lot of time with Alec, a Cameron Highlander, who had been a sniper hidden high up in a tree in Italy during the Second World War. The three missing fingers on his right hand was his most obvious wound, only his thumb and pinkie remaining.

"I hadn't blackened out my gun properly," he told me when I'd asked him how he had lost his fingers, "and I was spotted by a German sniper. Bang. That was it." He paused for a few seconds. "The guy was good at his job though," he said matter-of-factly. "He killed a lot of my pals, so I was pretty lucky only to be wounded."

Another individual who coped stoically with constant adversity was Hugh Mac, as he was known so as to distinguish him from another two patients on the same ward, both also named Hugh. Semi-paralysed on his left side, and with his left arm amputated from just below the elbow, he had received these wounds during the Korean War. Serving with the Royal Tank Regiment, he was the only one of his crew to survive and escape from his burning tank after being hit, albeit losing an arm and sustaining multiple other injuries which he would have to live with for the rest of his life.

In the six years that I knew them, I never heard Hugh Mac or Alec complain once.

Because these men - kids almost, at the time - went through what they did, it meant that I was of a generation who didn't have to go through it too, and I'm very often thankful for that, more than I ever let on to anyone.

If I were to tell Michael, Alec, Hugh or any of the other approximately three hundred patients, all of whom I once knew, and almost every one of them now sadly passed, about most of the problems and crises faced by us professional musicians, I can only imagine the incredulous response it would elicit. Probably nothing more than a slight derisory laugh followed by a raised eyebrow and a look of "You seriously think that that's an actual problem?", although I do also know that these men whom I've mentioned would have been too polite ever to do so.

I'll say it again, though. It's only a very few players who exhibit this behaviour.

It is in stark contrast to the overwhelmingly vast majority who are very nice, extremely honest, hard-working and amazingly highly talented people.

I remember being told during my days at the Academy, that out of all students of music, only the top five percent will actually get a full-time orchestral job, and I believe that figure is still the same today. To say that the competition for jobs is fierce would be an understatement indeed. Positions are advertised worldwide and players from around the globe will sacrifice a lot in pursuit of a permanent position.

Moving to another country and often even having to learn another language, leaving their family and all their friends behind and many more sacrifices are quite common, just so they can be in a professional environment which allows them to follow their passion.

This vast majority have a fantastic work ethic and will turn up for work through thick and thin.

I'm still very happy to go to work every day and I still enjoy being around them, in every orchestra with whom I play.

Chapter Eight

What a Show, There They Go, Smokin' Up the Sky

On a more upbeat note....

I briefly mentioned earlier the SNO's tour of Japan in October 1987, which to this day is by far the best tour I've ever been on. The BBC SSO's 2014 tour of India comes in at a well placed second, but Japan '87 was just outstanding in every way, and every other player who was there at the time says the same too.

We played in stunning concert halls and to a full and appreciative house each time, from Tokyo's famous Suntory Hall to the acoustically-acclaimed Yubin Chokin hall in Hiroshima. We went there playing via Osaka, Nagoya and Kyoto, the old Imperial capital, and then flew back up north again, past Mount Fuji to Chigasaki, around sixty kilometres south west of Tokyo.

We stayed in five-star hotels in which I never could afford to stay in real life. One of the hotels was brand new, having only been opened for six weeks and had a small stream - an actual stream diverted from a nearby larger one outside - running through the marbled lobby, complete with pond plants and live carp.

It was hectic leaving every venue's stage door because of the throngs of autograph hunters of all ages, waiting for the orchestra.

"Autograph? Me? Are you sure?" It was probably one of the very few times that someone's said "Do you know who I am?" with an inverted meaning and a puzzled expression.

And we got to travel on the Bullet Train, at that time the fastest train on the planet.

The culture shock was exquisite. I absolutely loved every second of it and I said at the time "One day I'm going to live here". I genuinely meant it then, and it's still on my to-do list now.

An added bonus was that the tour was conducted by Neeme Järvi, the Estonian maestro who is another of the very few conductors for whom I have the utmost respect. In fact, out of every conductor with whom I've ever worked, I'd say that he's probably my favourite, but don't tell anybody I said that.

Although he didn't talk anywhere near as much as some ego-centric conductors, he somehow often managed to just under-rehearse things, resulting in the orchestra having to give their complete and undivided attention to him during concerts, which invariably caused a few near-nervous breakdowns, but always produced outstanding results and tangibly electric performances.

I was excused the first two weeks of my post-graduate year (in the newly-opened RSAMD building) to go on that tour, helped by the fact that both of my teachers would be on it and as such, I wouldn't be missing any lessons anyway.

With the inspirational Gibbo on timps, the percussion section for that tour was Pam, Starky, Elspeth Rose (the SNO's lovely and wonderful full-time Third Percussion), and two freelance players - myself and Ian Coulter.

Ian was also Principal Percussion with the Scottish Ballet Orchestra and when the rehearsals for Japan arrived, it was one of the first times that we'd met each other.

We hit it off immediately and got on so well that it only took him another two years to ask me to play with the SBO.

When he did eventually book me for my first Scottish Ballet tour in autumn 1989, I jumped at the chance, mainly because it was Stravinsky's 'Petrushka,' a ballet score which includes fantastic and challenging percussion writing, excerpts of which are almost always asked for in orchestral percussion auditions world-wide.

The fact that I would also be surrounded by ballerinas for a whole month had absolutely no bearing whatsoever on my decision to accept Ian's kind offer.

Just thought I'd make that clear.

At six feet three 'and a bit' inches, and with a shock of red hair and red beard, Ian was mainly known as 'Big Ian', unsurprisingly, and still is today. Over the next twenty-plus years we would end up spending more time together than we did with our respective wives/partners, and we've both used the old adage that 'we'd have been out sooner for murder', but always said with affection of course.

This tour of Petrushka would involve a couple of weeks in Glasgow and one week each in Aberdeen and Newcastle, and would include one of the rare times that the percussion section had to be split between two locations.

His Majesty's Theatre in Aberdeen has what's referred to as an 'open pit'.

This means that the orchestra pit isn't underneath the stage as is normally the case, but is instead in front of the stage, with the orchestra in full view of the audience. As this particular pit is fairly small and the orchestra for Petrushka is fairly large and therefore space is at a premium, the four-person percussion section had to be split between its usual position and the Royal Box directly above it.

Ian and the lovely Debbie Garden were downstairs, and the equally lovely Louise Paterson was my colleague with me in the box above them, with the added bonus of a great view of the stage for a week.

Our section's 'usual position' in HMT is in reality, actually pretty unusual.

On each side of the HMT pit there are two small areas which resemble a couple of boxes as used by the audience, but free of any seating. The one on the pit-right side is home to the SBO's long-time timpanist Pete Evans and his four drums all tightly squeezed in.

Opposite this box and across the pit from Pete is the area the percussionists inhabit and we're even more tightly packed than Pete is in his space. In the past, there have often been up to four players crammed into this little box, along with a large orchestral bass drum, glock, xylophone and a lot of other UP. It's lucky that we all get on so well together as we're practically sitting on each other's laps for the week.

It also has a very low ceiling with one solitary light, of which even the shortest of us has to be wary when we stand up to play.

The light has, since day one, sported a lovely little glass shade in the shape of a bluebell and painted with a bunch of red flowers around it's outside. Admittedly, it's not really to my taste as it's more in the style of something my dear old gran would've gone for. Anyway, somewhere in the theatre there must be a ready supply of these shades because over the years I personally have destroyed two of them with over-zealous cymbal work and I know big Ian has despatched at least one.

Also taking up some precious space in our box is a large radiator.

It's an ornate, cast iron contraption that looks like it has been there since the theatre was built in 1906, and is constantly on, even when we turn its almost rusted-stuck mechanism to the 'off' position, and this has two effects on our section.

Firstly, it plays total havoc with our calf-headed bass drum which, when tuned, never stays at the sound it's just been tuned to, but instead rapidly dries out and quickly ends up sounding like a high-pitched tom-tom much to the consternation of whoever is unlucky enough to be playing and trying to control it at the time.

The second effect it has is of a more physical and longer lasting nature, though. By that, I mean it usually causes second degree burns on the nether regions of at least two unsuspecting players every tour, who receive a semi-permanent reminder to not bend over for any reason at that particular spot in our box.

Not only that, but added to the overall discomfort, we are almost totally walled-off from the rest of the orchestra which means that we can't hear anything apart from ourselves as soon as we start playing. We also have to constantly be in all manner of weird playing positions to be able to see the conductor through one of the two small windows incorporated into the wall.

The other window occasionally does have a use as well.

Prokofiev's score of 'Cinderella' requires the excruciatingly deafening twelve chimes of midnight to be played on a large bass tubular bell tuned to A-flat. The long, cylindrical bell itself is around eight feet tall with its supporting stand another few inches added to that and obviously much too tall for our low-ceilinged box in Aberdeen.

The only way around this problem is to place the bell outside of our box and in the pit itself but still within reach, so it usually ends up right next to the double bass section. They always enjoy telling me at every available opportunity how much they love that painfully loud bit of the ballet, as they've never had any use for their sense of hearing anyway.

The percussionist playing the bell part is still trapped inside the percussion box though, and on each of the twelve strikes, he appears through the little window to reach across the gap and play it, like a demented, hammer-wielding, tooled-up cuckoo, much to the amusement of those players in the rest of the orchestra who happen to be facing us, usually the violins.

Open pits can sometimes present their own unexpected problems and the pit in His Majesty's did this in quite spectacular style one time in particular, with an actual catastrophe narrowly averted, mainly by the strength of a male ballet dancer.

In the past, I've met a few professional footballers and ruby players who've been dragged along to the ballet by their wives or girlfriends and have surprised themselves by ending up being in awe and admiration of the strength and power of the dancers, especially the males.

Almost every theatre's stage is built on a slight slope, known as a 'rake'. This means that the front of the stage (nearest the audience) is lower than the back of the stage, and hence the terms 'upstage' and 'downstage'. This is unnoticeable to the audience, to whom the stage appears flat, but it serves its purpose by improving the overall view and sound of whatever production is on it at the time.

The stage at HMT has quite a steep rake and it's only been in recent years that they've attached a narrow net along the edge of it to catch anything that rolls off and into the pit, whether it's a tennis ball, an empty pretend wine bottle or a drunk actor.

In one of SB's productions of Romeo and Juliet, there's a scene where all the villagers from both factions of the Montagues and Capulets have a pitched battle. This really just involves all the *corps de ballet* huddled in equal numbers on each side of the stage shaking their fists and chucking bits of plastic fruit at each other.

Strength, beauty, finesse and control aside, dancers tend not to have full facility of their object-throwing capabilities for some reason, and a lot of the fruit, instead of hitting their sworn enemies, ends up either wedged in - and ultimately melted by - the lighting rig above the stage, thrown into the wings behind themselves after a premature release, or landing in the orchestra pit, in the form of a colourful, fruity meteor shower.

Most of the strings play this number huddled over their instruments to prevent any possible damage and a massive insurance claim.

Insurance questionnaire: Describe the cause of the £50,000 damage.

Answer: *Hole in violin caused by flying plastic banana.*

During one of these numbers in Hull New Theatre, which also has an open pit, the conductor looked over angrily at me when he heard a loud bass drum note, played randomly in the middle of the tune.

It wasn't me, though, because at that point I was in fact sitting beside the instrument with my arms crossed and watching a plastic orange, thrown obliquely by one of the boisterous Montagues, come sailing through the air towards me and ricocheting off the exact centre of the bass drum with a loud comedy 'BOING!'

Back at His Majesty's Theatre in Aberdeen, we were in the middle of our 1997/98 winter tour of 'La Fille Mal Gardée' and playing to full houses as it was a ballet popular with families.

With what I'd describe as twee and dreary music, composed by Ferdinand Hérold and arranged by John Lanchberry, it features a Clog Dance by a man in drag.

This is without a doubt my least favourite of all the ballets I've played.

'Napoli', a ballet by an amalgamation of four or five different little-known composers features the whole *corps de ballet* playing tambourines throughout and referred to by the orchestra as 'a bloody racket', comes a close second as my least favourite.

Napoli might have badly played tambourines, but La Fille Mal Gardée has clogs and a bloke dressed as a woman, criteria which elevate it to the undisputable number one spot on my 'worst ballets' list.

However, this SB production also has a pony! A real live one too, in every sense.

There were actually two ponies, cute little light brown Welsh Mountain Ponies each one taking it in turns to make an appearance in alternate shows.

The SBO's sub-principal second violin at the time, Liz Bailey loved horses and was overjoyed when she found out that we'd be touring a couple of live ponies.

I got on well with Liz, and liked her a lot, as she had a really good sense of humour and a big smile to match her 'big' blonde hair that was nearly always in a natural, almost-bouffant style which made her always recognisable, even from behind and at a distance.

Liz turned up early for every performance of this tour, just so she had time to visit the ponies in their little temporary enclosures, and at every interval in each performance she'd do the same.

As soon as the break started, she'd quickly put her violin away and go straight down to see the ponies, giving them lots of cuddles, patting and polo mints. The ponies really seemed to enjoy it too and one in particular - Liz's favourite - would get excited when she arrived, throwing its mane around and would always go straight over to her.

This was all innocent fun, until the second performance in Aberdeen.

Around halfway through the first act, Simon Stewart, one of the more experienced dancers, entered from stage left, dressed like a stereotypical eighteenth-century farmer, complete with floppy hat and casually chewing a stalk of wheat like all farmers do, apparently.

He slowly led on one of the ponies - Liz's favourite on its first performance of the week - which in turn was pulling a little cart with the pantomime dame Mother/bloke sitting on the back of it, feet dangling off the edge.

Then all hell broke loose.

As they neared the centre of the stage, and because it was an open pit for the first time on the tour, the pony spotted Liz's unmistakeable hairdo from behind, immediately got a massive erection and made a bee-line for her, almost tearing the leading reins from Simon's grasp.

It threw Kenny the Mother off the cart and sped towards the pit, as the steep rake helped it gather momentum.

All the parents in the audience quickly covered their children's eyes, shielding them not only from the impending bloody carnage, but also the rather disturbing, post-watershed sight of the pony's newly acquired giant pink fifth leg.

We - the percussion section - watched in horror and slow motion, our colleagues who were at that point still playing and facing away from the stage and therefore oblivious to it all, seconds away from becoming human bouncy castles for a horny midget horse and its cart, now racing towards the pit and about to be launched onto them from a great height.

Welsh Mountain Ponies were often bred to be used in coal mines, so they're not exactly weaklings, but Simon gave a great account of himself, and proved that all the money his parents had spent on ballet lessons for him had been well worth it.

He grabbed the pony around its neck, fighting against the rake of the stage and the love-struck pony itself, and although he was being inexorably dragged towards the pit, managed to hold it up just long enough to give five or six other dancers time to rush over and help, eventually directing and dragging the over-excited pony offstage and into the wings.

No doubt for a cold shower and a stern talking-to.

Chapter Nine

Dundonian Rhapsody

The Scottish Ballet Orchestra is without a doubt the friendliest and most sociable professional orchestra I've ever worked with and an orchestra of which I'm extremely proud to be a member. The friends that I've made there over the years are the type that, although life gets in the way and we don't see each other for long periods of time, when we do meet it's just like continuing a conversation from a few seconds ago.

Along with Big Ian, I mainly hung around with the brass section in those early halcyon days, namely Jon Clifford and Phil Nell, first and second trombones respectively, and the tuba player who's just about to make an appearance.

After Big Ian left the orchestra in 2011 to join the BBC SSO as assistant orchestra manager, things changed a bit for me personally as I took over the position of Principal Percussion after twenty-two years as Sub-Principal.

"With great power comes great responsibility," as the wise philosopher Spiderman's Uncle Ben said.

In my case, it was really more like "With an extra three pounds per show comes having to totally forget everything you've played for the last 22 years and learning to play completely different parts now," which I've managed to do with varying degrees of success.

I've been caught out a couple of times during shows thinking things like *"There should be some glock there. Why is no-one playing the glock?"* only to realise that I'm sitting in front of it and not any more at my old position on another instrument. *"Oh, it's me.... damn!"*

That would never have happened to my good friend, college contemporary and incredible player, the SBO's legendary Principal Tuba, Dave Dowall.

Dave D - yes, another Dave - left the SBO in 2000 after almost ten years there to take up the same position in the Ulster Orchestra, returning to the SBO again in 2004 until finally leaving in 2007.

One of Dundee's finest, Dave was not only tall, dark and handsome but was also one of the most intelligent and funniest people I've ever met. With the driest sense of humour ever, his delivery, sense of timing and unexpected one-liners always had those around him in tears of hilarity, very often during performances.

In Glasgow's Theatre Royal, the percussion section sits at the back of the orchestra pit as normal, and are right next to a pair of big, cumbersome metal pit doors which have a heavy black curtain in front of them.

These doors are facing the audience and open directly onto the brightly-lit backstage area, so once everyone in the orchestra is seated for each act, the doors are closed (normally by one of us percussionists) and the black curtain pulled across to stop any light flooding into the pit if the doors were to be opened again during the show.

During one particular performance in the early to mid-nineties, and before my self-imposed pre-show booze ban, I was sitting in my usual position next to the curtain and waiting to play the last few notes at the end of the first act and start the interval. I had about four or five minutes to wait and had done the ballet many times before, so I was sort of glazed over and daydreaming about something completely different which had nothing to do with ballet or music or anything.

You know how sometimes you get a strange feeling that you're being watched? Well, I got that.

I realise that by the nature of the job I do, there's a fair chance that I'm usually being watched by someone, but I can tell the difference, and sitting in the semi-darkness of the orchestra pit with the feeling that something spooky is watching you isn't too pleasant.

Three minutes earlier......

Dave played the last notes of his tuba part for the first act and put down his instrument as he'd done at the same point in every show for the past ten or so days. Because he couldn't be seen by the audience, he left the pit by a small single door in the pit-left wall behind Jon and Phil in the trombone section which also included Del Bishop on bass trombone, and headed for MacConnell's Bar, opposite the front door of the theatre.

The trombones, in between notes, each whispered their interval drinks order to Dave as he passed them on his way out of the pit.

"Large red.... PAARP!.... wine....."

"Pint of... PAARP!.... Guinness...."

"Double gin and.... PAARP!.... Tonic.... PAAARP!"

Dave got to the stage door and was about to cross an empty Hope Street to MacConnell's when he realised "Oh, I forgot to ask Marvin what he wanted!"

Dave called me Marvin, that one letter-change making all the humorous difference.

He turned around and walked quickly back down the backstage stairs and up to the pit's main, heavy double doors.

Dave could hear the music emanating gently and quietly from beyond the doors, so he slowly and silently turned the handle so as not to make a sound, stepped into the small space between the door and the curtain, and quietly closed the door behind himself.

Terrified of letting any light into the pit, he very carefully opened the curtain, but only a little bit at his head-height, one hand holding the curtain closed from a point just under his chin and all the way down to the floor. He slowly pushed his head through the gap, gripping the black curtain tightly around it, not allowing any light to escape into the pit.

He saw me sitting about twelve inches away and very softly whispered *'psssst....'*

No reaction.

Dave could see that I was staring into space and away daydreaming on another planet somewhere, so he said it again a bit louder.

'PSSSST...!'

That was when, in the half-light and my half-reverie, I turned around to see a massive disembodied head floating right next to my shoulder and hissing like a snake.

"AAARGHH!"
Whack!
"OUCH!"
I almost jumped out of my skin!
I got such a fright that I yelled loudly over the quietly playing strings, and because my limbs were now all flailing around of their own accord, I inadvertently and painfully whacked my ankle noisily off the snare drum's metal bottom rim.
I turned around again, wild-eyed, to see Dave's face quickly retreating back through the curtain and I heard it say "*Oh, bloody hell…!*" in quiet disbelief as it went, before it dissolved into hysterics that were thankfully muffled by the curtain.

✝✝✝

Scottish Ballet's 1995 Swan Lake tour was notable for quite a few reasons, one of which being that it involved the only occasion the show ran past it's three-hour running time and the whole company got paid overtime.
And it was all the fault of another band.
Or 'bands', to be specific.
Our four-act production - including the two intervals - lasted just three minutes short of three hours. The management were adamant that there was nothing that was going to prevent each performance starting on time, as it would cost a small fortune to pay the whole company overtime if it went even one second over the three-hour session, and we only had a tiny three-minute cushion if anything went wrong.
The Scottish Ballet technical crew under the directorship of George Thomson are without doubt one of the best in the UK, and they made sure everything went smoothly for the whole thirteen weeks, and each one of the seventy-two performances went without a hitch.
Except performance seventy-one.
The final day of the final week of the longest tour I've ever done.

By this time, every one of the dancers were continuing to dance through a multitude of injuries, and to this day I really have never seen anyone work as hard as a ballet dancer.

Also, by this time, almost all of the string players were taking regular painkillers and having massages to relieve the various aches and pains from playing their demanding Tchaikovsky parts on a daily basis, and twice a day on the two matinee days each week.

That might not sound a lot but playing a Tchaikovsky ballet is often compared to being the same as playing three Tchaikovsky symphonies in a row, and the strings are playing constantly. That's why I took up the drums.

The brass and wind sections were also struggling, having resorted to rubbing neat whisky into their embouchures to numb the pain of a thirteen-week-long hangover.

The final week of the tour was in Belfast, and on a beautifully sunny Saturday afternoon at the Grand Opera House, the first interval of the matinee performance arrived. The stage door opened and the vast majority of the orchestra poured out of it and quickly crossed the road to the famous Crown Bar which had been our second home for the week.

Even those in the orchestra who didn't really drink were there too, and there was a definite party feel in the air - we were in touching distance of finishing thirteen weeks of a long and difficult show, and all without major incident!

We had pre-warned the bar staff before the show and they had twenty-five or thirty pints of Guinness already waiting for us all when we arrived.

After a while, someone said "Three minutes to 'beginners'," (theatre terminology for a backstage call giving a timed warning for those people who are required to be in their positions at the beginning of an act) and so we all downed our drinks and exited the Crown.

About ten minutes later, back in the almost-deserted pit there were five musicians sitting in their respective seats and idly wondering where the other sixty were.

The other sixty were in fact still standing outside the Crown Bar and unable to cross the road because of the longest ever Orange Walk that had appeared while they were inside drinking Guinness.

If you are unfamiliar with Orange Walks, then by all means Google it, but don't stay there too long. I'll make no comment here about them, other than to say that I'm neither a fan, nor Roman Catholic.

What I will say is that no-one is allowed to cross between the bands on pain of severe injury or worse. Literally.

As it processed down the long, almost straight Great Victoria Street I looked along the length of the march, in the direction from which it had come and I couldn't see the end of it.

There were people still appearing into view as the Scottish Ballet Orchestra were standing outside on the pavement, stranded only fifty yards away from where they were meant to be. All the while time ticking on into overtime and the SB management holding up the performance, getting ever more panicked and furious by the second and still wondering where the hell their whole orchestra was.

***

A few weeks after that tour finished, Dave was sitting at home, polishing his tuba - and that's not a euphemism for anything - when his land-line phone rang and he picked up the receiver.

"Hello?"

"Hello, David. It's Evelyn Bryson here, Orchestra Manager at Scottish Ballet."

"Oh, hi Evelyn. How are you?"

"Not good, David. Not good at all, actually."

"Really? I'm sorry to hear that, Evelyn. What's the matter?"

"Well, David, I'll tell you what the matter is. I'm getting the orchestra parts for Swan Lake ready to go back to the company we hired them from, rubbing out pencil markings and bowings that were pencilled in for our production, and I've just got to the tuba part."

Uh-oh! thought Dave, as he suddenly realised what was coming.

Over the years, the multi-talented Dave has written quite a few poems - proper poems - and a few of them have actually been published in proper poetry publications. He let me read a couple of them once and I thought they were wonderful, especially one called 'The Fly'.

As the Swan Lake tour dragged on, Dave had become a little bit bored, and during one of shows he had written a limerick on the blank inside page of his tuba part.

Just a normal, inoffensive, slightly amusing five-line limerick.

However, as the tour progressed, his boredom increased exponentially with his colourful vocabulary, and by the end of the thirteen weeks, Dave had written almost fifty verses, using up every space on his music large enough to accommodate five lines of rhyming swearing.

What had started out as an innocent, gentle comment on the conducting qualities of one of our two conductors, slowly transformed over those fifty verses into something completely different and too graphic to print even here.

The only verse that is suitable for sensitive eyes is the one which I actually found to be the funniest by far. It appeared as an oasis of polite, creative comic genius in the middle of a tumultuous sea of hilarious tirade all directed towards the hapless conductor.

'His beats he thought were enhancers
For the orchestra and the dancers
But were always too quick,
At a hell of a lick
Like the Charge of the Third Bengal Lancers.'

Dave's sensational *tour de force* should have, in my opinion, been studied by schoolchildren the world over as the finest example of perfect humour, pace and creative swearing.

Sadly, though, it is no longer with us.

"So, here's what we'll do," said an audibly annoyed Evelyn down the phone. "I'll send you the tuba part and you can rub everything out, or we'll have to hold you liable for a complete set of new orchestral parts."

"Ok, Evelyn. I'll do that. Many apologies."

"Apology accepted, but don't do it again."

"No, I won't."

"Glad to hear it, David. Bye."

"Bye, Evelyn."

Dave hung up the phone and thought for a few seconds.

He lifted the receiver again and dialled, and the phone on the other end picked up after a couple of rings.

"Hello, Evelyn Bryson, Orchestra Manager at Scottish Ballet."

"Hi Evelyn, it's Dave again."

"Oh, hello. What can I do for you?"

"What we were just talking about…."

"Yes, what about it?"

"Well, when you send me the part for Swan Lake, could you also send me the tuba parts for Romeo and Juliet, Coppelia, La Sylphide and Sleeping Beauty?"

Then he added "But don't look at them."

Chapter Ten

Death by Tambourine

Like any self-respecting, neurotic musician, I have a couple of recurring anxiety dreams.

They usually make an appearance in one form or another around once a month, sometimes more, sometimes less but there's always one there, lurking in the background and ready to jump into my sleep, shaking it's unwelcome, sweaty jazz hands at me when I least expect it.

The first is a generic one common to most musicians.

I'm standing at the front of the orchestra as the soloist in a concerto that I've never even heard of, let alone practised. It's more often than not in a packed Albert Hall and I'm then handed an instrument I don't play, like a violin or a trumpet - and no, not percussion as some wags have said in the past when I've mentioned this. Just as the conductor gives the downbeat, ignoring my protestations, I wake up startled and sweaty and unable to get back to sleep for the rest of the night.

The dream I get the most often though, is a bit of a niche nightmare and involves the tambourine part of 'Petrushka'.

In real life, this is quite a difficult part and one passage in particular is always on the 'orchestral excerpts' list for any orchestral percussion audition. It involves a few different tambourine techniques in a fairly short space of time, the main challenge being the many 'thumb rolls' required.

Thumb rolls are executed by pushing the thumb or middle finger of one hand against and around the circumference of the tambourine's head ('skin' for the uninitiated) thereby creating friction, and this results in a constant buzz-roll.

I'm sure you'll be rushing off to buy a tambourine and practice this right now.

Anyway, that's not the main concern in my dream.

Towards the end of the piece, the puppet - Petrushka - dies, and to signify this the tambourine player is directed in his part to 'drop the tambourine on the floor.'

All week long, in my dream, the conductor has been on my case about this one note and how I'm not dropping the tambourine correctly. He's been furious at me across the orchestra at every rehearsal, shouting insults and berating me and I'm now determined to prove him wrong and get it right at the concert.

Once again, it's a packed hall somewhere, and the thumb-roll passage has gone brilliantly, with the 'drop' fast approaching.

The music is deathly quiet and I've managed to silently pick the tambourine up and move into a crouched position, holding the instrument two inches from, and level to the stage floor.

There's a short pause. The only sound is a quiet suspended cymbal roll and an almost inaudible held clarinet note.

The clarinet then plays a short upbeat into the first beat of the next bar and I drop the instrument on the second beat and become the solo, under-stated moment of death of Petrushka.

Perfect.

The solemn, gentle music continues and I silently stand up and slowly slide back onto my stool.

What a relief!

It was the best single note tambourine drop that anyone has ever heard, including the conductor who is now smiling across at me and nodding his head in approval and admiration.

I'm finished until the end of the piece now, so I'll just relax, cross my legs and enjoy the last few minutes.

That's when, as soon as I lift my right leg, I accidentally kick the instrument I've left on the floor.

The tambourine, with the power of dreams, makes the loudest 'BANG!' ever and shoots off like a clay pigeon, whooshing between the heads of the third and fourth French horns before violently smacking into the back of the head of one of the second violinists and ricocheting off a few more players in that section before coming to rest in the middle of the strings, spinning like a coin, faster and faster, louder and louder until it stops with a sudden 'zzrrrrch!'

There are bodies, blood and brains all over the stage and I once again wake up startled and drenched in sweat.

This one has always puzzled me why my pals copped it and the evil conductor escaped unscathed. Very strange.

In other dreams, I'm sitting at home watching television. Suddenly all the channels are simultaneously broadcasting the 'Concert of the Century', beaming it live around the world. It's five minutes before it starts and all of a sudden on the tv screen in my living room, there's a camera shot of my drum kit on stage, still in its cases and not even set up, and I realise I'm supposed to be there too, playing.

Dave Lyons also gets this exact same dream, strangely enough.

I have to mention here that I laugh every day at work. Not constantly, like a giggling buffoon, I hasten to add, but at least once every day, and always around Dave. We've known each other since I was sixteen and he fourteen, and we very much have a strange telepathy and can almost always tell what the other is thinking, and so I wasn't particularly surprised that he had this dream too.

And as another fellow colleague and friend, Rik Evans, said in his wedding speech about his Best Man - he's like the brother I never wanted.

Unlike me, though, Dave is the type of person that remembers every dream they have and can recount them daily.

I put it down to the over-use of all the tablets, pills, potions and weird balms that he's been self-medicating with for decades. It's only been in the last few months that Dave has stopped walking around like a portable chemist shop as he's suddenly realised, after years of me trying to tell him, that there's actually nothing wrong with him after all.

Except Irritable Bowel Syndrome.

He has always been more than happy to share news of his newly-acquired ailments, real or imagined, with us, whether we want to hear about them or not, and Dave's IBS gets name-checked on an almost-daily basis.

One particular nightmare that Dave had involved that very same affliction to one end of his alimentary canal and his attempt to proffer some temporary respite to the awkward irritation.

In this nightmare, Dave was in a large Morrison's supermarket not far from where he lives and had gone straight to the fruit and vegetable aisle. He picked up a couple of bags of mixed salad leaves and placed them in his basket before heading straight to the medicine aisle. These bags were being used purely for camouflage, and when he was sure that no-one was watching, he quickly picked up a large tube of Anusol, hid it expertly under the salad and made his way to the checkouts.

The store was busy and there were long queues at all the checkouts. Dave didn't fancy putting his shopping on the slow-moving conveyer belt and standing for ages with his Anusol on display to all those around him, so he decided to head for the self-service ones, where there would be a much less chance of anyone spying his potentially embarrassing purchase.

There was only one little unit available in the bustling area and he headed straight for it, placed his basket down and opened a plastic bag ready to surreptitiously accept the clandestinely concealed anal anodyne cream.

He nonchalantly reached underneath the two salad bags, picked up the long, rectangular box containing the tube of comforting rectal relief and scanned it across the glass-fronted reader.

There was no confirming little 'beep', so Dave scanned it again. Nothing.

He tried again. Still nothing.

He could hear the noisy, bleeping scanners from all around his unit all working away fine and was about to try again when he noticed a small orange light, flashing above his screen.

"Are you alright there?" said a voice from behind him.

He turned around to see a lady in a Morrison's uniform who, before Dave could move, had taken the box from out his hand and began trying to scan it herself.

"It's not scanning," she said. "I'll go and find out the price for you."

Dave, now quite a bit flustered, was about to say "No, it's ok thanks. I'll just leave it," but only managed to say "No, it's...." when instead of stealthily taking the item away and having it discretely priced, the customer 'helper' shouted over eight checkouts, all with long queues, to her pal at the checkout furthest away from Dave.

"Hey! Mary! How much for the Anusol?"

"What?" replied Mary, as everyone in the whole store turned and looked at Dave.

"I SAID, HOW MUCH FOR THE ANUSOL?! THIS GUY CAN'T SCAN IT!"

Now, when I said that this was a nightmare that Dave had, I meant that metaphorically.

It actually happened in real life.

If you're reading this to your children, which I sincerely hope you're not, then you might want to skip this next bit, because it may come as a bit of a shock to them as it involves graphic animal self-mutilation and grand deception on the scale of Santa Clause-gate.

The mascot, and face of BBC's annual charity mega-fundraiser, Children in Need (CiN) - Pudsey Bear - isn't in fact a real bear.

It is instead, although ultra-convincing and realistic to the touch if you're blind and with no sense of feeling in your hands, a guy in a yellow, one-eyed bear costume.

Dave L's second-best idea ever, after the stunning 'fountains coming out of the xylophone,' when we were students at the Academy, had the potential to propel Pudsey Bear to the heights of musical and percussive stardom to which luminary drummers, the likes of Karen Carpenter, Mr Bean and the Roland SPD11 drum machine could only aspire.

A few years ago, Dave had approached the BBC SSO's management with this particular idea and they seemed to be very impressed with it indeed.

"How about, at the orchestra's Children in Need family concert this year, Pudsey got to actually play the drums along with the orchestra? It would need to be done by a real drummer or it would probably just look stupid, so I could dress up in the costume and do it if you want?"

"Great idea, Dave!" said the management. "We'll do that, but you'll need to meet with the CiN team first and discuss the do's and don'ts of being in the bear costume."

So, Dave got the all-clear to appear as Pudsey on CiN day that November and beforehand, he met up with a Pudsey representative to go over the final details.

"It was like signing the Official Secrets Act," Dave told us later. "I had to sign a disclaimer containing a long list of things. Stuff like 'no speaking', 'no showing any indication of a human inside the costume', 'keep waving' - all that type of stuff."

The concert arrived and although a bit on the hot and sweaty side, Dave was doing well. Dressed as Pudsey Bear, he'd made his entrance to a cheering City Halls audience full of parents and children, waved until his arms were getting tired and hadn't said a single word so far.

All good.

"Would you like to see Pudsey playing the drums, boys and girls?" asked Jamie MacDougall, presenter of BBC Radio Scotland's 'Classics Unwrapped' programme and host for the evening's concert. Dave, myself and a couple of other players on the stage had known Jamie since school days, as a fellow member of the Strathclyde Schools Orchestra in which he was a violinist, before giving up music altogether and becoming an opera singer.

"YES!" screamed the kids.

Dave's 'handler' - one of the CiN team, dressed all in black to blend in with the rest of the orchestra - led him down to the drum kit, as Dave couldn't really see where he was going because of the ill-fitting costume, and sat him down in position, placing a pair of sticks in his giant paws.

The number started and Pudsey began to play, swinging along nicely with the orchestra until the middle section arrived, whereupon he put the sticks down on the floor of the stage riser behind himself, stood up and did some more waving to the children, just as he'd practised at the rehearsal.

He sat back down and turned around to pick his drumsticks up.

What Dave hadn't taken into account at the rehearsal though, was that he'd be wearing a bear head that he couldn't see out of, especially when sitting down and also that he'd be wearing a pair of large, fluffy, four-fingered bear paws with very little to zero flexibility.

He couldn't see where he'd put his sticks down only a minute earlier, and as he tilted his head up and down, rocking backwards and forwards to try and peer out of a little hazy, gauze-covered gap in the costume head's mouth, he gave the impression to the audience of a head-banging, mentally ill and possibly vomiting bear.

Just as the drums were about to come in again, Dave spotted his sticks and reached out to quickly grab them, only to discover that he couldn't pick them up because of the massive gloved paws on his hands which only served to push the sticks around in circles on the floor.

With his entry fast approaching, there was only one thing for it....

The children all watched in horror as Pudsey Bear ripped the skin off his own paws, revealing what looked awfully like a pair of spooky human hands and picked up his sticks, playing through what must have been agonising pain for a poor six-foot, one eyed, bipedal, ursine drumming maniac.

Some years later, in fact quite recently, I was on drum kit for a CiN concert but dressed as myself, thankfully.

The management of one of the big 'stars' that would be performing with the orchestra, a household name that suffers from a well-documented development disorder characterised by significant difficulties in social interaction, had given the BBC management a 'rider' - a list of things that sets out what an artist requires backstage either before, during or after their performance.

At the first rehearsal, which was for the orchestra only and without any soloists, the producer in charge of the concert stood on the conductor's podium and briefly addressed the band.

"Ladies and gentlemen," said the producer, "I can't quite believe what I'm about to say. When our soloist arrives for the rehearsal tomorrow, please do not go up and speak to them. We have to treat them very delicately, like a baby deer, otherwise they'll very likely freak out, run away and not come back for the concert."

Another of the BBC management team was standing beside me during this short announcement, and a player sitting near us pointed to me and said jokingly to him "So that means Marty can't creep up behind the soloist and honk one of those taxi horns the percussion use, then?"

"Don't joke", was the reply. "The rider we got from their management only asked for a bucket to be placed just offstage, as the soloist usually throws up with nerves just before going on."

I did genuinely think "Poor thing, that's a real shame!"

Then I thought "But it certainly beats asking for a giant bowl of M and M's with all the brown ones removed."

Eddie Gallagher *(left)* and **Eldon Byrne** outside **Hotel Colon** just before setting off for **Bar Eclipse** *(below left)*, **Madrid.**

Primal Scream. Genuine relief immediately after leaving **Bar Eclipse.**

The SBO percussion section and our view of the open pit, **His Majesty's Theatre, Aberdeen.** Only myself and Owen were in this pictured section for Nutcracker - imagine how cramped it is with two or three more players along with a lot more (and larger) instruments. Note the window on the left, used by the bass drum player to see the conductor, and the killer radiator just visible, bottom right.

Scottish Ballet Orchestra on tour, **Hull, England** circa 1992. *(l-r),* **Jon Clifford** (trombone), **Kevin Chapman** (piano), **Phil Nell** (trombone), **Dave Dowall** (tuba), **Ian Coulter** (percussion).

Border control, crossing from **Latvia** to **Estonia**, BBC SSO **Baltic** Tour, 1997.

The musician's river, **The Beautiful Blue** (Grey) **Danube.** BBC SSO, Germany and Austria, 1993.

Playing the actual lethal tambourine part for Petrushka, BBC SSO Prom concert at the **Royal Albert Hall, London**, 2016. I was pleased to report a performance with a body-count of zero.

The only way of getting the instruments into the concert hall - slowly and one at a time. **Troy, New York State,** BBC SSO tour of **East Coast USA**, March 2001.

Chapter Eleven

Mr. Ballet's Disappointing Night Out

In September 1994, Sir Edward Heath, the ex-British Prime Minister came to Glasgow specifically to conduct the Scottish Ballet Orchestra in a one-off Gala fundraising concert.

It was all arranged at the very last minute.

The Chief Executive of SB at the time, Peter Kyle knew Ted Heath and so had invited him at short notice to conduct the performance. Having such a world-famous person adding their name and support to Scottish Ballet could only be a good thing, and all the management were very happy indeed when Heath accepted the offer.

The sponsor of the concert was one of the SBO's double bass player's father-in-law, who owned a whisky export business at the time and was trying to break into the Chinese market, and saw a great opportunity here, what with the many possible contacts of a true British elder statesman.

The whole thing was arranged at such short notice that we only had time for one three-hour rehearsal on the day of the concert, but as it was a programme of ballet music, we were all pretty confident it would be fine.

The orchestra would be in full view, seated on the Theatre Royal's stage and not in the pit, our usual home, with just enough space at the front of the stage to accommodate two dancers who were both soloists with the company. They would dance the *Pas de Deux* from 'Nutcracker' and 'Swan Lake' amongst other numbers.

Before the rehearsal started, one of the SB management addressed the orchestra.

"Ladies and gentlemen, thank you for helping to bring this concert off at such short notice. The only thing to clarify is that the dress for tonight's concert is black dinner jackets for the gents, and fancy dresses for the ladies."

Normally, the ladies would be asked to wear 'ball gowns' or 'evening dresses' or something along those lines and not 'fancy dresses', which sort-of means the same thing but avoids any possible confusion.

'What possible confusion could that cause?' I hear you ask.

Well, the Principal Flute misheard and she turned up for the concert with Sir Edward Heath that evening, dressed as Rupert Bear, complete with yellow checked scarf and a cute, drawn-on little black nose.

According to the bastion of all humankind's knowledge, Wikipedia, 'Heath was a keen yachtsman' which he was pretty good at, to be fair and also 'maintained an interest in classical music.'

'Maintained an interest'....

Without wishing to appear mean-spirited towards the amateur conductor, he did try his best, but he was a politician and not a professional musician. Even though he conducted a Christmas Carol concert every year from his teens onwards (says Wikipedia), that didn't necessarily qualify him as being able to conduct a full-blown concert of well-known ballet music which is a lot more complex than Christmas carols, and unfortunately, he struggled with every number we played.

The orchestra's leader at the time was actually 'conducting' each piece from his violin and everyone in the orchestra followed him instead, and not Sir Edward. This was actually a 'first', as the whole orchestra usually tried their best to ignore this particular leader when he was playing.

There was one non-ballet piece on the programme for some reason, which was Prokofiev's 'Peter and the Wolf,' and it was narrated by the Scottish music hall local legend Jimmy Logan.

Before the concert began, Jimmy had found the backstage supply of the sponsor's product and had thought something along the lines of *'Oooh, free whisky! I'll just have one very small one....'*

So, by the time Peter and the Wolf appeared in the concert, Jimmy was totally sozzled and slurring through the words, sometimes having to repeat sentences, as he'd read them wrongly the first time.

"DON'T SHOOT THE BIRDIE!" Peter said to the Hunters at one point, with dram-fuelled dramatic flair and making no sense to the story whatsoever. "Oh, sorry…. Er, I meant 'DON'T SHOOT! Birdie and I have caught the wolf!"

I don't know how much was raised, but I do know that the sponsor's company went bust shortly afterwards, although I'm sure it was nothing at all to do with Jimmy Logan and the amount of their stock that was consumed that night.

As you're now aware if you weren't already, conductors are important. The best ones just get on with the job with no histrionics and are generally respected by us cynical musicians. It's usually the mediocre ones who make up for their lack of talent with supreme confidence and arrogance and of course, we can spot them a mile away.

The conductor with whom I've worked the most over the past thirty or so years is Scottish Ballet's Richard Honner. He started at SB three years before I did and is still there.

Here, Richard eloquently explains the unique differences and challenges faced by ballet conductors over the years, compared to conductors of symphony orchestras or opera.

Richard Honner - Head of Music, Scottish Ballet, and conductor for SBO 1986-present,

Late in November 1985 my telephone rang. I knew of the caller, the then Music Director of Scottish Ballet; although we had never met, we had mutual friends. "I was wondering whether you would be free to conduct performances of *The Nutcracker* in January, and of course whether it would be of interest," he asked. "Of interest yes, but I know nothing about dance." My slight acquaintance with ballet was while I was on the staff at Covent Garden – it was possible to sneak in to watch Royal Ballet stage rehearsals and I had on occasion taken the opportunity to obtain passes to the staff box for Saturday matinees. However, I had never really been bitten by the terpsichorean bug. "Not to worry, let's meet and discuss things," he responded. Thus, a few days later, with permission granted from Scottish Opera, I was taking scores of *The Nutcracker* home and with the aid of Andre Previn's recording I was on a speed learning course as there was little time left before I was to watch the dress rehearsal in the Playhouse in Edinburgh. I discovered that there was a wealth of wonderful music not included in the familiar *Nutcracker Suite*, like the last twenty minutes of Act 1, a span of music so inventive and colourful I was amazed. Things must have gone reasonably well with the handful of performances I conducted as I was invited back for a triple bill in the spring and then offered a permanent position from August 1986.

Part of my job specification as the second conductor was playing for daily class, something for which I didn't have a natural aptitude, as twenty years as a repetiteur in opera companies had made me reliant on the printed page. However, with some advice from a sympathetic member of the Ballet Staff, and years of experience I managed just about satisfactorily, but without the sparkle and imagination that a really talented class pianist can display. I was, however, much more comfortable with playing for rehearsals as my experience as a repetiteur had also made disregarding the printed page and creating a credible pianistic rendition of orchestral scores second nature. What this close, daily relationship with the dancers taught me over many years was to understand the nature of dancers' movement and how good choreography sits snugly on the music. Unlike singers who have some control over the speed and shape of the accompaniment, dancers are totally dependent on the support and sympathy of the musicians in the pit. They trust the conductor implicitly.

Over the years, through the reigns of successive Artistic Directors, Scottish Ballet has embarked on a zigzagging stylistic journey from 19th century classics through to specially commissioned works. We musicians have had the opportunity to perform a very varied repertoire from Adam, Delibes and Tchaikovsky to John Adams, Cole Porter, Webern, Mahler, Britten and new scores by Eddie McGuire, Peter Salem and Robert Moran. It is more than likely that I would never have come to know much of this music and for that I am grateful. To have had the chance to conduct *Romeo and Juliet* more than three hundred times in six different productions has proved a joy – it is surely the most eloquent, dramatic and colourful score ever written for the dance stage.

The conductor for ballet must undertake different responsibilities from his colleagues in an opera company or a symphony orchestra. The latter two set all the parameters for the musical and dramatic performance but in ballet the end result is a compromise made by all performers, arrived at by a process of trial and error, and finally negotiation. This might sound like an abnegation of musical responsibilities but after thirty years of working in ballet companies, the most satisfying artistic experiences have been those performances where the most discussion, and sometimes pain, have been part of the creative process and where all parties buy into the final concept. The ballet conductor therefore has added challenges, to ensure that the performance matches the vision agreed upon during rehearsal in terms of tempo and dramatic pace, that the dancers feel supported and loved and that the orchestra is persuaded that the way the performance is being shaped is convincing to them, and thus ultimately to the audience. This might mean performing well known numbers at unexpected speeds (which could mean finding a different way of phrasing or playing to those which a concert orchestra might adopt) or by employing an unexpected sense of *rubato*. The ultimate test is whether the music supports the visual production and therefore any musical quirks are seen to be convincing. In addition, one should aim to provide a satisfying musical performance for a member of the audience who may have decided to close his or her eyes.

The best way of developing a role in the ballet's creative process is to play the piano for rehearsals. Often one ends up playing pas de deux (usually the most detailed and difficult movements to accompany) dozens of times during a rehearsal period. By the time the orchestra arrives the conductor has the pace and the musical shape of these movements in his or her bones. It is very similar to the old system in opera companies where conductors rose through the ranks from a junior coach to a senior repetiteur and then onto the rostrum to take over performances from a seasoned colleague. Most of the great twentieth century conductors followed this path. Knowledge of the repertoire is accrued, wisdom of the tricks that make performances work are absorbed, can be tried out and yes, may eventually be jettisoned with experience. Tradition is sometimes decried as laziness but equally it might be the most convincing way to build a performance. I am glad that I spent twenty years in opera companies slowly working through the ranks and similarly thirty years in ballet companies. There is just no alternative to that sort of training. In these days of instant results, young conductors do not expect to put in the hours of unglamorous repetition that the rehearsal process demands, and I fear that as a result many of the solutions to awkward moments in performance will not be learnt and therefore the problems will not be solved satisfactorily.

One of the great lessons a ballet conductor needs to absorb is to temper his or her ego, instead investing that energy in the common concept. That is not to say that one should not have ideas about how the music should go under ideal conditions - the composer's vision should always be the starting point - but with the proviso that matters might change with necessity (choreographic or technical) and one should not be daunted by this. A challenge is stimulating. One of the problems I encountered when I joined Scottish Ballet was the lack of a common language between the artistic staff and the music staff. Words like *anacrusis* or *tempo*, bandied freely about in a discussion laden with dance terms left one struggling to understand the nub of the problem. That sort of misunderstanding coupled with my inexperience led eventually to my suggestion of setting up a course with the Royal Conservatoire of Scotland for young pianists wishing to enter the dance world. Too often I had seen new pianists experience the gulf between their own musical understanding and the expectations of the Ballet Staff. Confusion and frustration led some to ultimately throw in the towel. By offering support, experience and the passing on of knowledge in much the same way as used to happen for young pianists in opera companies, we are developing a more sophisticated dialogue between dancers and musicians which might eventually offer to some a path to the rostrum, thereby raising the status of the ballet conductor in the eyes of the musical world. Being a musician associated with dance has long been perceived as a second division occupation, below that of an opera or concert conductor. My experience has taught me that conducting for dance is every bit as complicated and demands just the same sensitivity and commitment.

In 1992, a couple of years prior to the Sir Edward Heath concert, Alan Barker became Scottish Ballet's Music Director, with Richard as his second-in-command, and stayed in the post until 2006.

Barker, a small-statured Australian of rotund frame was an archetypal Ballet conductor. He had been around for a long time before joining SB, and the list of people he'd worked with read like a who's who of famous dancers and choreographers, with the likes of Margot Fonteyn, Rudolf Nureyev, Natalia Makarova, Mikhail Baryshnikov and Georges Balanchine decking out his *Curriculum Vitae*.

I liked Alan Barker, and I think that the rest of the SBO secretly did too, although most of us did decry his conducting technique which often resembled a man picking up and throwing an invisible toddler over his right shoulder on the first beat of every bar.

Being an Aussie, he had that Down-Under charm mixed with unexpected Digger coarseness, which I found to be very funny indeed.

In rehearsals, one of his favourite expressions was used - often - to indicate that the orchestra could be a bit tighter musically in certain passages.

"Ladies and gentlemen," he'd charmingly say, as he stopped the orchestra. "We're not together at all." There would be a few nods of agreement from various players and Alan would qualify it by saying "Yes, it's all over the place, like a mad woman's shit. Ok, let's go again from figure twelve."

Some of us could push his buttons a little, and took a little twisted pleasure in doing so, especially when we deliberately referred to him as our 'Musical Director'.

"I'm the *MUSIC* Director!" he'd rage. "I don't direct fucking Musicals!"

Previously, Barker had studied under John Lanchberry, who was, amongst many other things, the arranger of 'La Fille Mal Gardée', and whom he'd idolised and always spoke of in revered tones, calling him 'Mr. Ballet'.

Lanchberry once came to Glasgow's Theatre Royal to see his protégé Barker conduct another of his ballet arrangements, 'Two Pigeons' by André Messager (arranged Lanchberry).

Barker had been visibly twitchy for days and became ever more nervous and irritable as the performance in question approached. The score wasn't particularly taxing for the orchestra, so he didn't want us to then become complacent because of it, and before every performance leading up to the one that his tutor would attend, we would find numerous Post-it notes stuck in our parts with various instructions about the music from Barker, and we could tell it was a big deal for him, Lanchberry being one of his idols.

The production of Two Pigeons involved two live white doves onstage, who would be starring in the title roles of the pigeons.

They symbolised the two eponymous lovers and were provided by 'the man who trains the parrots in Edinburgh Zoo', apparently.

Sitting each on their own perch, one on either side of the stage, the pigeons didn't have a lot to do, to be honest. At a particular point in the show, one pigeon had to fly from stage right to the perch on stage left and join it's 'lover' and they both then sat there until the end of the short ballet.

During the show though, when the bird got the signal to go, it flew off its perch, went straight upwards and disappeared, enjoying a nice, warm seat on the lights above the stage. The other one on stage left spotted its pal fly away, so it decided to do the same and joined it. They both did this in every performance, and each time, the trainer would spend some time with the birds afterwards and then say "I think I've sorted it now. The next performance should be fine," but it never was.

As the Lanchberry performance arrived, the whole orchestra was called to a meeting backstage prior to it and we received a pep-talk from Alan, rather like a teacher speaking to their class of remedial primary school kids before the School Inspectors arrive. "Now, as you're all aware, Mr Ballet is coming tonight. I want total concentration from everyone for the entire show and best behaviour, ladies and gentlemen. And trombones - that includes you lot too."

7.30pm arrived, the house lights went down and Barker made his entrance into the pit to the applause of a full auditorium.

The conductor's podium was placed quite high up because the Theatre Royal's pit is deep and the conductor has to be able to see both the orchestra down in the pit and the dancers up on the stage. The three steps up to the podium were in fact three wooden boxes, fashioned by the SB technical crew and had been in use for years, with a one hundred per cent safety record so far.

The boxes were quite big though, which forced the conductors to take slightly higher steps than they normally would.

You can probably tell where this is going now....

As the applause died away and Mr Ballet sat back in his seat to enjoy the fruits of his labour and the technical prowess that he'd passed on to his hard working and diligent student, Barker went to step up onto the final box but didn't step quite high enough. His foot slipped off, and his weight and momentum made him instantly disappear underneath his music stand with a loud and painful clatter.

He immediately jumped back up, completely shaken and reappearing with his spectacles at a jaunty angle like Captain Mainwaring from 'Dad's Army'.

Taking everyone by surprise, he flicked his baton in a sudden, strange, half-downbeat movement that we'd never seen the likes of before, and with the only thing missing being a shout of "*Expelliarmus!*" he started the ballet before everyone in the orchestra was ready.

Some players came in. Some others came in and stopped, then came in again, unsure of what was meant to be happening, and others didn't play at all.

It was all over the place, like a mad woman's shit.

Eventually the music got itself under control somehow, and the rest of the performance went without further incident, until the pigeons went skyward again, but that at least was expected, and the whole episode was never mentioned by Alan ever again.

Chapter Twelve

Certa Cito

'*T*ECHNICAL problems yesterday silenced what should have been the first major coup of the BBC Scottish Symphony Orchestra's epoch-making tour to China.*

The BBC SSO's performance at Shanghai's International Festival of the Arts was meant to have been transmitted live to Britain, but technical difficulties left Radio Three listeners in the UK listening to recordings of the orchestra yesterday morning.

The radio broadcast, a central plank of the network's New China season, was abandoned only minutes before the concert began when the satellite link failed to connect.

After two days of work by sound engineers had traced the initial breakdown to a failure at the Grand Theatre itself, the cancellation eventually came about because of a problem with the downloading of the signal at the UK end.

In Shanghai itself, the orchestra played for the second night to a capacity house and the inclusion of Aaron Copland's wartime salute to US democracy, Lincoln Portrait, received a stunned then enthusiastic response.

It was notable, however, that a party of state officials who had arrived together by coach was less appreciative of the work.

The rarely-performed piece, previously recorded by Prime Minister Margaret Thatcher and US General Norman Schwarzkopf, includes some resonant lines for residents of the most Westernised of China's cities.

The audience was enthralled by the narration of Giles Havergal, artistic director of the Glasgow Citizens' Theatre, which was translated into Chinese characters on super titles above the stage. Quoting the 16th president, the text proclaims: "The dogmas of the quiet past are inadequate in the stormy present. As our case is new, so we must think anew and act anew. This nation shall have a new birth of freedom."

The response to the words - and the rousing score - overshadowed the following performance of Beethoven's Fifth Symphony, an established local favourite.

Only the rows of Communist Party cardholders, identifiable by their red lapel badges, and a few other scattered individuals were noticeably less enthusiastic at its climax.

The concert was the second date of the BBC SSO's tour, both of which have been very warmly received in Shanghai and both of which have been recorded, now for future transmission on the BBC music network.

Speaking after the concert, orchestra director Hugh MacDonald said of the failure of the live link: "It is very sad because people put a lot of effort into a very difficult arrangement logistically. I suppose it is just one of those things, but it is very disappointing."

The technical team travelling with the band on its debut tour of China was told only 48 hours before the planned broadcast that the necessary permissions were not in place from the Ministry of Culture of the People's Republic.

By the time the government in Beijing had agreed to the transmission, contingency plans were already in place for UK listeners to hear Saturday night's concert in place of the scheduled performance.

That emergency exercise would have involved producer Simon Lord taking the recording of the Saturday concert, which featured a different programme and is scheduled to be broadcast on Radio Three on Friday, to the BBC's offices in Hong Kong and relaying it back to the UK. Inquiries had already been made about flight availability before the administrative difficulty was resolved.

The Copland piece was specifically requested by the festival promoters after they heard the orchestra play it in Wells Cathedral at the Bath Festival.

Its performance marked not only the centenary of the birth of the composer, but it also, by uncanny coincidence, fell on exactly the same date in the calendar that Abraham Lincoln delivered the Gettysburg address in 1863.'

- The Herald, 20th November 2000

In November 2000, the BBC SSO became the first Scottish orchestra to tour China and Taiwan, and the first Western orchestra to play in the Great Hall of the People in Beijing's Tiananmen Square.

A BBC camera crew that came along to film a documentary of the historic tour for BBC television followed us for the whole time, but at the very end of the tour, missed out on something that would have, without question, been the highlight of the TV programme.

The above piece that appeared in the Glasgow Herald newspaper the day after the second concert in Shanghai's Grand Theatre, gives a small insight into some of the backstage difficulties and technical challenges that face the various 'support' teams that without whom, no orchestra would be able to function.

At a concert, the audience only sees the people on stage, and although I'm sure that they're all aware that unseen others are involved in the running of the concert, it's not really something the vast majority of the paying public would fully appreciate. Anyway, the backstage crews and management almost always say that if the audience are not aware of their input to the performance and they've remained invisible to them, then they've done their job well.

The RSNO's Stage Management crew are an absolutely incredible duo. Not only are Craig Swindells and Michael Cameron constantly working, but they always deal with everything with great humour, professionalism and pride in their work. Nothing is too much trouble for them and however much these guys are paid, it's nowhere near enough.

Another of these unsung heroes is a man whom I've known for almost my whole professional career. He is the instrument truck driver for the BBC SSO and like Craig and Michael, is as professional, talented and meticulous in his work as any musician in that orchestra, and for whom he is responsible for ensuring their hundreds of thousands of pounds-worth of instruments arrive safely on time at any given venue, worldwide.

Allan Hannah is immediately likeable. Strawberry blonde-haired with a manly moustache to match and a strong East-coast Scottish accent, he is an absolute gentleman.

Allan is the type of person who is always extremely helpful and will try his utmost to accommodate everyone.

Players are always asking him to transport items of theirs, things like luggage, golf clubs or bits of furniture they've bought before a concert somewhere and need it transported back to Glasgow, and although he has an endless ton of work to do and gear to shift, load and unload, Allan will always try his best to help others.

When I had the first notions of writing this book, three stories immediately sprung to mind. Actually, they didn't 'spring to mind' but were, in truth more or less the instigators of the whole project.

Two of these three were both stories involving Allan, and both illustrate perfectly some of the things that happen behind the scenes, and are incidents that not only the audience, but in some cases the players themselves are not aware of, and the extent of commitment by some people to make sure the concert starts on time.

Allan was one of only three people who were aware that I was writing a book originally. This was because, after a London Prom concert in July 2017, I had asked him if I could possibly 'interview' him about these two incidents and wanted to be completely honest with him regarding its purpose. He very kindly said 'yes' and also very kindly agreed to keep it a secret, which is exactly what he did, and something I'm very grateful for. I didn't want anything leaking out to other players that I was even thinking of writing something.

We had talked a lot in the past about these incidents, and about his previous life in the British Army, but I wanted to get it all down properly, so we arranged that I would visit Allan at his house in a small town near Bathgate, where he said he would answer my questions as best as he could.

Allan picked me up from the station and when we arrived at his house, he put the kettle on as I set up my GoPro and also the video on my phone as backup, so that I could get everything word-for-word, and not go making up what I thought I'd remembered he'd said, so the following is verbatim from the man himself.

He told me that the best times for him were in his army days, where he served with the Royal Corps of Signals and amongst other things, qualified as a Combat Driver. This is an extremely difficult achievement, and only a small percentage of those who attempt the course will actually make it.

"I had my Combat Driver's test along with a Colonel from the regiment, a Sergeant-Major from the regiment and a Captain from the regiment, and I was a Corporal. That was three commissioned officers - they all failed and I passed. That was some day! I've got a big certificate for that, too," he said and then smiled. "It was hanging up on the wall until Bernie (*Allan's wife*) took it down because she was fed up looking at it."

Allan's military career came to a sudden end when, at the height of the Troubles, he was wounded in Northern Ireland.

Like many soldiers before him, he is very private about a lot of things that happened during his time with the Royal Corps of Signals, and I have no intention of breaking the trust that he has shown to me by writing anything that he's asked me not to, and I'm sure you can appreciate that.

The BBC SSO have toured China three times to date - in 2000, 2008 and 2014.

On the first tour - the 16th to 29th November, 2000 - and after almost ten days in China, the orchestra had the final concert of the tour in HsinChu city, about eighty-five kilometres southwest of Taipei, the capital city of Taiwan.

The Chinese stipulated that the orchestra had to use Chinese drivers, so Allan would travel in a separate government-provided car and in convoy with either two or four trucks and have overall responsibility for the equipment they were transporting and all the corresponding paperwork.

In November 2000, after playing in Beijing, Shanghai and Guangzhou, we had a travel day and flew to Taiwan for the final concert of the tour.

The next day, rumours started spreading around the players that the concert that night was going to be cancelled. Everyone's first reaction was to treat it as the usual rumour someone has started out of boredom, and no-one took it seriously.

But as the day wore on, the rumour grew and when the management cancelled the rehearsal and postponed the coaches' departure time to the venue by an hour, we suddenly sat up and took it seriously after all.

Apparently, there was some problem with the instrument tucks, but they were on their way and so we would wait at the venue for them to arrive.

And so, we turned up, without any instruments, at the venue.

It was a basketball stadium which had been transformed into a concert hall for one evening only. By 'transformed' I mean that the hoops and backboards had been swung out of the way and the orchestra was placed on the court, surrounded on three sides by the audience.

It wasn't long now until the 7.30 start and still no sign of the trucks. Everyone was milling around and throwing in their two cents-worth in the "will it happen - won't it happen?" debate that was now the only topic of discussion going on.

It was highly unusual for the Taiwanese to have a Western orchestra play in their country, so this was a pretty big event, making it another sold-out concert and the audience were now arriving in droves, quickly filling up the stadium. We could see the management in great turmoil, having to possibly make a monumental decision whether to cancel the concert at the last minute or not.

Just after 7.20pm, the orchestra management breathed a huge sigh of relief. "The trucks are here!" they said, almost shouting it with joy. "Percussion, get your gear set up as quickly as you can. Actually, do it quicker!"

We did it and were ready with less than two minutes to spare, and the audience were none the wiser.

What were the reasons behind all of this? I asked Allan, and with something that would not be out of place in a James Bond movie, he replied with the following;

After the concert in Guangzhou and I'd got the trucks loaded, I went back to the hotel where we were all staying, and had an early night because I knew the next day would be long. The next morning, the orchestra were leaving to fly to Taiwan, and my luggage went with them because I had to clear customs with the instruments and then go with a later flight. But when we went to customs in Guangzhou at nine in the morning, they decided to give me a 'turnout'. They wanted everything off the two trucks, and so I had to get them onto a loading bank.

The Chinese truck drivers were not allowed to touch anything, so I had to take everything out from the trucks myself, and I had it all laying out across this banking. Customs would then come up and they'd pick a box and then ask me to open that box and take all the stuff out.

They came to the timps, and they wanted me to take the skins off the timps so they could see inside, and I refused point blank. I said 'That's not going to happen'.

So then, they had me taking the double basses out. Now, the double basses are in their soft covers, and then they're in their hard flight cases. I had to take them out the hard cases, then take them out the covers so that they could examine everything.

All this took several hours, so the plane that I was due to get - it had gone. So, after they [customs] were all happy, having checked all the instruments, et cetera, they then wanted me to load the trucks back up, which I again had to do myself.

I then gave them the paperwork to clear customs.

The paperwork I had was a photocopy, and that was a problem. They refused to accept a photocopy and wanted the original documents.

So, by this time, I've had to get on the phone and phone over to Taiwan to speak to Alan Davis, the orchestra manager. Alan Davis then said he would have to get in touch with people [promoters] in

Shanghai, and they'd get somebody from Shanghai to fly down to Guangzhou and told me that I was to meet them.

So, I was to meet a Chinaman in Guangzhou airport?

I said to Alan "That's going to be practically impossible. There'll be about three million Chinamen there." But I was told that this one was quite tall and had long hair. So, I said, "That'll narrow it down to about a million." However, we made an arrangement that the Chinaman would find me because I was the one with ginger hair and I'd be the ONLY one that was in there with ginger hair. And that's what happened.

When he arrived, we jumped in a taxi to go back to the customs, as he now had all the original paperwork that we needed.

[*What time was this now?*] Well, the customs shut at five o'clock and this was just after four o'clock. The flight had arrived into Guangzhou at about 3.50pm from Shanghai - it's only a half-hour or an hour flight, something like that - so it's now just after four o'clock and we're in a taxi coming out of the airport to head towards the customs place, where I'd been all day.

We then got into a gridlock and there was no traffic moving in either direction. The only people that were moving were the people on motorbikes, going up the side of all the taxis and the rest of the traffic.

So, we decided to jump out of the taxi and we hijacked a motorbike each.

We took the motorbikes off the guys, told the guys where we were going - obviously the guy from Shanghai explained that we were going to the customs.

We got into the customs with two minutes to spare, just before the five o'clock deadline, and we got the paperwork stamped.

Then it was a case of getting everything from Guangzhou to Hong Kong.

I was to meet an agent in Hong Kong who was going to take the details of all the instruments to get them onto a plane to Taiwan. So, I got all that done - went from Guangzhou to Hong Kong, gave the details to the guy and went back to Guangzhou.

The orchestra were already in Taiwan but it turned out that I had to stay overnight in Guangzhou and then leave first thing in the morning and go and clear customs at Hong Kong and put the stuff on the aeroplane.

So that's us now into another day, and it's on this evening that the concert was due to start.

So, we got the plane to Taipei and we met people there - there was a truck there, pre-arranged, and the flight got in at five o'clock at night. It was a two-and-a-half-hour drive to the concert - I can't remember the name of the place - but it was a basketball stadium.

I bribed the truck driver to drive up the hard shoulder to get up there in time. So, he was doing that, when the motorway was choc-a-block he was going up the hard shoulder and overtaking everything. We got there, got the truck unloaded and set up, and the concert went ahead with about five minutes to spare.

Yes, it was all quite hectic.

Back in Guangzhou, I'd had no clothes to change into because all my gear was already away with the orchestra, so I made arrangements with the hotel for them to launder my clothes. They sent a maid up to collect all my clothes, launder them and have them ready for five o'clock in the morning, and that's what she did - and that was spot on.

That meant I had clean clothes for starting the second half of the journey, because I had to get the train from Guangzhou to Hong Kong - it's just a short journey, about half an hour or so.

When I got to the venue in Taipei, I was absolutely shattered, and I remember the concert had started and I found a wee corner at the back of the stadium and just crashed out, so I never heard any of it. I was out cold.

When we went back to the hotel, I explained everything to John McCormick *(Controller of BBC Scotland)*.

John McCormick said "I wish we'd had the cameras with you when you hijacked the motorbikes. That would've made good television!"

[*How did the actual hijacking come about?*] We just opened the doors of the taxi, and the first bike that came along... knocked the boy off the bike and took the bike off him.

[*Did you say anything to the guys?*] It happened that fast. We told the boys - well the guy from Shanghai told them - where we were

149

going and at what time, and that the motorbikes would be left at this place, at customs and excise, so we never ever heard from them again.

[*So, they must have got the bikes back?*] Oh, they definitely got the motorbikes back, yes. When we got to Customs and Excise, we got a taxi from there to get back to the airport but we told Customs and Excise that these motorbikes belonged to these specific guys.

But that's the only reason we made it with two minutes to spare. Two minutes!

Otherwise, the concert would have been cancelled. We never would have made it.

The first Western orchestra to play there!

After the concert, when we got to the hotel, Hugh MacDonald came up to my room and said "I need you to come downstairs, Allan" and I said "No, I'm going to my bed, I'm tired." Obviously, the next morning was going to be another challenge, getting back to Hong Kong with the instruments, etc., and I said "No, I don't want to go".

Then, shortly afterwards, one of the players came up to my room, and said "You need to come downstairs", and I said "I've already had Hugh Macdonald up and no, I'm not coming down. That's it - finished". He said "The orchestra wants you to come down", and I said "I'm not coming down!"

Then somebody else came up - I think it was Graeme Taylor, the sound engineer who said "Allan, you need to come down" I said "I'm not coming down, I'm tired. Let me sleep!" but I gave in and I went down, and as soon as I arrived [in the room], the orchestra formed a big circle, and I had to go into the middle of it, and that's when John McCormick gave me the presentation.

You know, I've still got that presentation there, unopened, still in all the packaging and the bow tie still wrapped around it, and everything else still on it.

I was nearly crying when I got that presentation.

We were the first Western orchestra to play in the Great Hall of the People.

That was an experience as well, because I had sixteen guys and every single one of them was five feet tall - there was a dead straight line of heads. We had four old-fashioned trucks and there were four guys to each truck, and when we arrived at the Great Hall, the guys were taking the instruments out and they were running up the steps with them. I had to get in touch with the interpreter and say "look, tell them to walk - don't run". He said "They're only trying to be helpful". I said it'd be more helpful if they just walked. We can't afford to have any damages to the instruments. And the wee guys, they couldn't speak a word of English. All I got was "Yes, Boss" and "No, Boss."

To me, the Chinese people [I dealt with] on the first trip - because Taiwan had broken away from mainland China - were deliberately making life difficult as we were leaving their China to go to Taiwan.

But it was a case of persevering. There were times, going from, say, Beijing, Shanghai or flying from different places, I would come up against people at the airports who would say "We're going to put your instruments on two airplanes" but I insisted that all the instruments travel together on one airplane, and they would say "We don't have enough room", so I would say "Well I'll just get another agent" more or less, things like that. They were looking for a bribe from me which I wouldn't give them.

The airport at night.... it's like a cattle market. I actually witnessed men coming out of big, fancy cars, with pin-striped suits and big wads of notes.... they needed a pallet taken somewhere here or there.

In this one instance, I could see the plane that I was supposed to be going on with the instruments, and this guy appeared with a wad of notes - he'd bribed the airport people, and this pallet was to go on the plane too. That's when they told me that they were going to put the instruments on two planes and I refused point blank. I said "All the instruments go on the one plane." So, I stuck to my guns and it worked.

Streetwise - you've got to be streetwise in China.

There's a lot that goes on that the orchestra doesn't know anything about. They only see when they get off their coaches that their instruments are there, waiting for them and they've no idea what went through getting them there.

Anyway, that was the first trip.

On the next China tour, in 2008, we were going from one province to another province. All the instruments were in two trucks and I was in an official government car.

Now, the guy I'm travelling with, he is responsible for the province that we're going to but he had no jurisdiction in the province that we were in. So anyway, it was about two o'clock in the morning and we were driving up a country road - pitch black - and all of a sudden, two Land Rovers overtook us and the blue lights came on and they stopped us.

There were four policemen in each Land Rover. They got out, sub-machine guns, etc. and the first thing they did was to go into the two trucks and pull the drivers out. Then they went into the cabs and threw everything that was in there onto the ground. They [the police] had great big beam torches - big, big torches.

The two drivers were told to stand at the side of the second lorry. So, the government official and I, we're standing separately from them, but then the government official goes to join the other two drivers.

So, I picked up my briefcase to go as well.

The next second there's two sub-machine guns stuck right into my ribs, and it was obvious that I wasn't to go anywhere.

So, I'm now thinking 'are these real policemen or are they bandits?' because the area we were in was bandit territory. And then I'm thinking 'are they going to shoot them [the drivers] or are they going to shoot me? Is it an inside job? Is the government official involved in all this?' And all these things are going through my head.

So, I decided that I was going to go into the briefcase and get paperwork to show the captain of police. I went down on my knees, into the briefcase on the ground and immediately got another two submachine guns stuck in my ribs.

That's four guns now.

I can remember looking up and seeing that one of them was a young guy, and the sweat was running off him. It was actually dripping onto me, and I said to myself, 'if this guy panics, I'm dead.'

By this time, I'd got the documents out but I can't see anything because it's pitch black, so I've now got to get up onto my feet and get to the front of the truck to use its headlights to find the paperwork I need.

So, I go through the paperwork, and I've missed the bit I need.

I go through it again and I've missed it a second time.

Now, I'm beginning to panic. Normally I'm quite calm, but I'm beginning to panic.

The third time, I got the document that I needed and I gave it to the captain of the police. It was the authorization to go from the province we were in to the province we were going to.

The captain of the police read it, stood to attention, gave me a smart salute and - in perfect English - told me that we were free to go. And all the time, when I was trying to talk to him in English, he wouldn't listen. He knew all along.

The next day, I went down into the city of Shenzhen and [points to left forearm] I decided to get this tattoo with my name in Chinese characters, so that if somebody was going to shoot me and throw me in a ditch, someone else would come along and see my tattoo say "That guy's name is Allan Hannah."

And that was the reason I got it.

Chapter Thirteen

Bim Rings

wesome.

Now, there's word that's had its fundamental meaning watered down to such an extent that it's now just a mere shadow of its former self.

It's defined as;

Extremely impressive or daunting; inspiring awe. (Late 16th century) - *Oxford Dictionary*

Or, for Oxbridge balance;

Causing feelings of great admiration, respect, or fear - *Cambridge Dictionary*

The power of Nature, manifested in a volcanic eruption, earthquake or tornado for example, is awesome.

The testament to human ingenuity embodied by the technology, engineering and utterly devastating firepower of a Boeing Apache helicopter in action is awesome.

The chicken vindaloo I had for dinner last night was not awesome.

Admittedly, it was very nice and I'd probably go back to that particular restaurant again, but to be pedantically true to its original meaning, it wasn't awesome.

The word is almost always mis-used nowadays and to be honest, I'm just as guilty of that as everyone else.

There are some occasions though, when I do use it in its original form and quite often it's to describe a colleague.

Even after thirty years of playing mainly the right notes, I still feel extremely privileged to be doing the job I do.

One of the many reasons for this is that every day, when I turn up to work with any of the orchestras, there are usually one or two people who - purely by their playing and mastery of their instrument - make it an absolute joy for me to be there.

Not every orchestra has them, but there are a few players who, through their musicianship, sound and instrumental proficiency, stand out from an already (mostly) highly-talented crowd.

Players like Martin 'Gibbo' Gibson (timpani), Stella McCracken (oboe), John Gracie (trumpet), Janet Richardson (piccolo), Alberto Menéndez Escribano (French horn) and the Scottish Ballet Orchestra's beautiful Principal Flute, the incomparable Jo Shaw.

I could go on.

These incredible players really are an inspiration and I have nothing but great admiration for their outstanding musicianship.

I absolutely adore their playing, and so by these criteria, they are indeed awesome.

They are all solo players, which means that they are the only person playing their particular line in the music. This obviously makes it a lot easier to determine if someone is good or otherwise. It's much more difficult to hear individual string players when there's ten of them playing an identical melodic line and trying to figure out which one of them is a stand-out (or otherwise) player.

In autumn 2014, I was asked to play Stravinsky's 'L'Histoire du Soldat' (A Soldier's Tale). The septet of single instruments would be made up of mainly BBC SSO players, with myself from SBO and there would be two performances. The first one would be a concert for the BBC SSO Club, sometimes referred to as the 'Supporter's Club', and both would be conducted by Martyn Brabbins, the ex-BBC SSO's Associate Principal Conductor for twelve years from 1994 and still a regular face at the front of both the BBC SSO and RSNO.

Written during the First World War and premièred in 1918, it's based on a Russian folk tale and is the story of a soldier who gives his violin to the devil in exchange for a book that predicts the economy of the future.

It's a challenging piece for all the players, involving constant changes of time signature, and so it's almost always performed with a conductor.

In September 2017, Martyn Brabbins was back again, conducting the BBC SSO for a week of Tippet Symphony no.3, a difficult piece to play and also pretty difficult to listen to.

Just before we started one of the rehearsals, he said to the orchestra "I thought that this year was the twenty-fifth anniversary of my first time conducting you lot, but the office has just informed me that it's actually the twenty-sixth year. They also told me that, including this week, I've done nine hundred and thirty-three pieces with you."

There was a few "ooh's" and "aah's" from the players and a small applause which Brabbins cut short by saying "So, I'm really sorry about that," which got a hearty laugh from the players.

One of the main things about Martyn which has always impressed me is the way he copes with rapidly changing time signatures with remarkable ease.

His concerts with the BBC SSO have been heavily marked by contemporary works - whether by design or not, I have no idea - and in all these years and in all these pieces, his beating has been impeccable and I have never seen Martyn Brabbins put a wrong one in. In particular, all the weeks of his, in the early years, which have contained works by Messiaen spring to mind.

As players, when we look down at our own parts and look back up again at the conductor, it's quite shocking how many of them are totally lost and on the wrong beat of the bar - even the 'big names'. This is immensely confusing to the players and often results in players unnecessarily adapting to where they think they should be in their parts but should actually have just ignored the conductor and continued doing exactly what they were doing because they were right in the first place.

Fast, complex changes on every bar seem to be Brabbins' *forte* and he has been constantly rock-solid and utterly reliable since day one. With a very pleasant character and a demeanour which never comes across as aggressive in any way whatsoever, I have always found him a pleasure to work with and he is the final addition to my grammatically incorrect 'Top Three Conductors That I've Worked With'.

If you can't be bothered searching through the earlier pages to find the other two, the list is, in no particular order - Martyn Brabbins, Ilan Volkov and Neemi Jaarvi.

All three are very different and uniquely distinct in their styles and personalities, but they are the only conductors whose weeks I look forward to being involved with.

Anyway, back to 'Soldier's Tale'....

By chance, Martyn Brabbins was working with the BBC SSO in the week that the first performance of 'Soldier's Tale' was due and kindly agreed to direct it. Like the other six instrumentalists' parts, it's a tricky little multi-percussion piece for us percussionists but I was very happy indeed when I heard that Martyn would be conducting.

The whole work is very much violin-led, with a concerto-like part and needs a violinist of virtuoso level to be able to play it well. The piece lasts for an hour, so for the violinist it's really more like playing two or three violin concertos in a row.

This was the first time I'd heard Barbara Downie play solo.

Barbara is in the second violin section of the BBC SSO and sits there, not quite anonymously but with another eleven making up the section, her seating position changing on a weekly rotational basis with eight others, and with the whole section generally playing the same line.

I've always had a lot of time for Barbara. Dark-haired and very pretty, with the gentlest of personalities and a quirky sense of humour that I totally love, she always makes me laugh. Although Scottish, she studied in America and had previously worked with the Houston Grand Opera and the Houston Symphony Orchestra, based in Texas. I had known this already and had therefore assumed she was pretty good anyway, but until I actually heard her play on her own I'd no idea just how good a musician she was.

At the first rehearsal for Soldier's Tale, I was completely blown away by her virtuosic playing - she was just incredible.

Awesome, in fact.

It made me briefly wonder that maybe all second-violinists were in fact secretly world-class soloists that just preferred an anonymous life in an orchestra section.

It's always possible.

Apart from his skill with rapidly changing time signatures, the other thing that has always impressed me about Martyn Brabbins is his ability to ask individual players an innocent question to which the answer almost certainly causes great spontaneous hilarity, intended or not.

I've always thought that trumpet sections are very often the generic 'geeks' of the orchestra. And by that, I don't mean it in the sense that they're 'weedy' or weaklings in any way. The RSNO's wonderful Sub-Principal Trumpet, Marcus Pope served in the Parachute Regiment, for one example, and the SBO's equally wonderful Sub-Principal Trumpet, Alan Friel has run dozens of half-marathons and - in his own, typically modest words - "only" three full marathons, for another example of trumpet manliness.

What I mean is that they are the section most likely to take their instrument and all of its associated paraphernalia to the extreme. Every section has some players who live and breathe their instrument, but the trumpets as a collective whole are definitely way ahead of everyone else in that field.

They arrive at work, wearing bandoliers full of mouthpieces, ready to swap them with each other in the same way that kids used to swap football cards at school, sit down and get their instruments out. They then proceed to open large rucksacks that they've each brought along, out of which they pull bizarre contraptions that look like they could only have been acquired from an Anne Summers' bargain bin. They're always weird-looking plastic things with various connected rubber tubes which they blow into - *senza* mouthpiece - as they check gauges, or little windows on the outside of the machine through which can be seen a tiny floating polystyrene ball, just to see if their breath control has improved any since the day before.

Sometimes the trombones join in for a bit, but they get easily bored, and so usually don't keep it going that long, preferring instead to discuss the merits of real ale, and which particular one they'll be sampling as soon as the current rehearsal/gig is finished.

In the early to mid-nineties, the trumpets' favourite fad was the Bim Ring.

I have to confess that I didn't know its original name, and even after extensive research, I'm still unsure of whether it should be capitalised or not.

However, I think it's a brilliant name, so I've therefore decided it deserves capitalisation and also to be mentioned as often as I can fit it in.

The Bim Ring was a fairly large and heavy brass disc with a hole in the centre, through which the trumpet mouthpiece was inserted prior to it joining on to the trumpet itself, and at one time it seemed like every orchestral trumpeter I saw was using one (a Bim Ring).

I asked Robert Baxter and Brian McGinley - two of the best freelance trumpeters in the country and both top blokes indeed - about Bim Rings, and both of them ended with the same sentiment, independently of each other.

"They're called 'Bim Rings'" said Robert. "And I think I know why you're asking" he added with his trademark cheeky smile.

"Those particular (big round) Bim Rings have gone out of fashion a bit" Brian said, "but there are more 'normal' looking ones you can get now (which are unfortunately no longer called 'Bim Rings'). They're basically a way of adding more mass and acoustic dampening to a point on the instrument. Loads of companies make them now and most are called 'sound sleeves' or 'mouthpiece weights'. You get similar things for the bell, but they make it much more dead sounding. At the mouthpiece end they can feel more 'solid', but don't have the same ring to the sound. It's basically a preference thing! By the way, are you thinking about what I think you're thinking about?"

So now you and I officially know what a Bim Ring is.

And yes, they were right about what I was thinking about...

Nigel Boddice was the BBC SSO's Principal Trumpet from 1975-1995. In twenty years sitting in that 'hot seat', he played hundreds of concerts and broadcasts, if not thousands, all over the world to millions, if not billions of people and blasted trillions, if not gazillions of notes at them.

Although, that's not the first thing that springs into my mind, or anyone else's if they were at a certain rehearsal in 1993 - or indeed any brass player in the country when someone mentions him, because a lot of these notes Nigel played in the later years were even more focussed and weighty with the help of a fabled Bim Ring.

During this particular rehearsal at the height of the Bim Ring craze, Martyn Brabbins looked up at the trumpet section and with a puzzled expression and furrowed brow, stopped the orchestra.

A trombonist himself, Brabbins had never seen one of these things before and, intrigued, he asked "Nigel, what's that on the end of your trumpet?"

Before Nigel had time to reply, the Second Trombone answered for him, in his distinctive, jovial North-East of England accent, which - phonetically - sounded like "A big, fat coont!", and has since gone down in the annals of legendary replies to a conductor.

So, that's:
Orchestra - 1
Maestro Brabbins' Innocent Questions Answered - 0

But the score is about to change....

Another rehearsal with another orchestra....
Martyn stops the orchestra again.
He studies his score, with a furrowed brow and looks up at the percussion section, unsure which one of us is playing the specific Latin American instrument, the erroneous rhythm of which he would like to check, and to great amusement, innocently asks the notoriously barking mad, highly-strung percussionist "Annie, are you bongos?"

You can usually tell something's not quite right if a seventy-piece orchestra all shout "Yes!" as one.

Orchestra - 2
Maestro Brabbins' Innocent Questions Answered - 0

Dave Lyons has the loudest ever pair of Glockenspiel beaters.
Not acoustically loud, but visually loud.
Utterly eyeball-meltingly deafening.

He has a pair of luminous yellow Glock sticks that have missed out on their true calling. I don't know where he got them and I really should have made the effort to find out the actual make of these sticks before writing this, because I have never seen anyone, anywhere with a similar pair.

They have distracted me in rehearsals and concerts a multitude of times already, mostly just by catching sight of them in my peripheral vision when they're sitting on a trap tray doing nothing, and always when Dave is using them in action....

They are so lustrous in their shining radiancy, that whatever chemical compound was used to make them so blindingly luminescent should also be used, in my opinion, in everything else incandescent in today's modern world.

Motorway cat's eyes, hi-visibility jackets and the universe's incalculable quasars are all insipid, pale and ghostly achromatic in comparison to these things.

As dazzling as they are though, they sound totally dull and absolutely terrible.

Really, really bad.

I know Dave agrees with this, so all is fine that way, but....

....in one rehearsal....

Martyn Brabbins stops the orchestra and, with a furrowed brow, studies his score for a bit.

He looks up at the percussion section, but this time he can see which instrument each one of us is playing.

"Dave," says the maestro in a diplomatic tone, and continues... "I don't like that 'dark' sound you're getting from the Glock. Have you got any brighter sticks?"

To give Dave his due, he just held them up, blinding the whole orchestra and said "Er...no, not really."

Orchestra - 3
Maestro Brabbins' Innocent Questions Answered - 0

This next bit needs a brief explanation first.

There are a few pieces which require a siren, played by one of the percussionists, and there are a number of different types of siren.

Firstly, there's the old-fashioned hand-cranked type that one would see in movies, usually set in the Second World War, and it produces a low howl which slowly *crescendos* to a high-pitched scream the faster it is cranked and warns of approaching bombers.

There's also a small, silver instrument resembling the bell of a trumpet that, when blown, produces a high pitched, comical "wheeeeee!"

Then there's another one similar to the first but instead of being hand-cranked, it's electrically wired up to a power unit, and the volume and pitch is controlled by a knob which is turned in the same way as the volume controls found on amplifiers or stereo systems.

If the type of siren hasn't been specified, the hire company will usually send to the orchestra one siren of random choice, either hand-cranked or electric, along with a little silver one.

There was a player who, to be very diplomatic about it, was not particularly worldly-wise. In fact, even to this day they can be described as extremely naïve and really wouldn't know a sexual innuendo if it offered to take them for a short trip and rummage around a Lady Garden with a lovely view of a French hedge.

They also had a little quirky habit of adding the word "job" to everything, for example:

"Which snare drum shall I put up for the rehearsal?"

"It's Scheherazade, that's always a Premier job" meaning the Premier branded snare drum should be set up, as opposed to the Tama or Pearl ones belonging to the orchestra.

Or sticks could be - and have been - described as "wooden jobs" or "nylon-tipped jobs". I'm sure you've got the idea.

Martyn Brabbins was once again in Glasgow, conducting a programme of contemporary music which featured Edgard Varèse's "Ionisation", a piece for thirteen percussionists, ground-breaking when it was written and the big finisher of the concert.

As we were setting up the instruments before the first rehearsal, we opened the large flight case full of weird instruments that the hire company had sent us from London and amongst it all we found two sirens - an electric one and a small silver one that I really didn't fancy putting anywhere near my mouth. I was a bit put off by the greenish-brown colour of its little mouthpiece, a cross between the colour of a stagnant pond and the inside of a prison cell which housed a disgruntled felon in the midst of a dirty protest.

"Martyn!" shouted my colleague, from the back of the stage, which was thankfully empty apart from a few drummers setting up their own gear, to Brabbins, who was standing on the conductor's podium at the front. "Which siren do you want?!"

Martyn looked up from studying his score, a little distracted. "Sorry, I was miles away, what was that?"

"I said," came the yelled reply without any irony or basic social awareness whatsoever, "DO YOU WANT AN ELECTRIC JOB, OR DO YOU WANT A BLOW JOB?!"

The rest of us were just relieved the hire company hadn't sent up a hand-cranked one as well.

Chapter Fourteen

Like Chess, But With Puncture Wounds

*"I find that fencing and training give me more stamina and help me
deal with the craziness of being on the road so much."*
- ***Bruce Dickinson,*** lead singer with **Iron Maiden**

"**M**usic is my religion."
Jimi Hendrix said that.

Although I wouldn't go so far as to say it was my religion, I can see
where he was coming from.

I'm not by any means suggesting that music isn't important - far
from it. Music is extremely important for a great many reasons.

For a start, it's a fundamental cornerstone of human communication
and has been since humans first existed. It's been well documented
that early humans made a kind of singing noise to communicate
before the evolution of speech. How they discovered this, I've no
idea but it certainly seems to be the case.

Orchestral music has sometimes been hijacked by those trying to
make it the preserve of the elite classes, which I believe is absolute
hypocrisy - all music is for everyone!

Every single composer throughout the ages has written their music
to be enjoyed by everyone, from the man and woman in the street to
royalty. It didn't matter to them which social status people belonged
to, they only wanted to write their music to be played and heard.

A major example of this is the phenomena of "El Sistema".

Translated as "The System" and founded by José Antonio Abreu, it was established in Venezuela in 1975 to provide free classical music training for the country's most impoverished children.

Abreu said that "Music has to be recognized as an agent of social development, in the highest sense because it transmits the highest values – solidarity, harmony, mutual compassion. And it has the ability to unite an entire community, and to express sublime feelings."

El Sistema has been called "The most important orchestral and social project in music history" and has official partner programmes around the world, namely in the USA, Canada, Portugal and the UK.

Scotland has adopted an El Sistema programme, called "Sistema Scotland" and at the time of writing, currently engages with over 1,800 children from three of the most deprived areas of the country.

And although it's not my 'religion', music is one of the major facets - if not THE major facet - of my life.

The world of orchestral playing is without a doubt, a highly intense one, and I don't want to give the impression of anything otherwise.

I am just as susceptible as the next musician to being caught up in various mental torments, lying awake at night and worrying over minute details of things I could have played better, or upcoming difficult repertoire.

As players, we are in a constant state of being judged by others in everything we do, every day, every rehearsal, every note, and although it's not a literal life or death situation, it is very often not a pleasant environment in which to live and work.

It all takes place in the bubble of Orchestra-World - a phrase popularly thought to have been coined by Frank Zappa after his fractious dealings with the LSO when recording his works with them in the 1970s - and removed from the realities of the "real" world.

Things like being asked by conductors who are experienced enough to know better, to play Tchaikovsky's "Nutcracker" ballet in the style of Mozart (*WHAT?!*), along with changing the massive climaxes in its *Pas de Deux* from their original emotionally-charged *triple forte* to an insipid *mezzo-forte* "because there's only two people on stage" (*SERIOUSLY?!*) causes a mixture of derision and an instant loss of any respect for the conductor that the orchestra may have had at the beginning of the rehearsal.

Yes, it's a rather misguided, uninformed and frankly idiotic thing to ask, but it's not exactly walking into a burning building to save someone's life, knowing full well that you could very easily forfeit your own but still doing it anyway, as my father did on a daily basis in his job.

He joined the Glasgow Fire Service on 4th October 1963, when Glasgow was known as "Tinderbox City" due to the amount of regular, devastating fatal fires it experienced in the 1960s and '70s. After twenty-nine years in the service he'd gone from the rank of Fireman to Assistant Divisional Officer and is still extremely proud of his time there, just as I am of him.

Something that helps to counter the Orchestra-World pressure a little - for me - is that I've always been lucky enough to have had other interests outside of music.

Some friends and colleagues have no interests apart from music, and that's fine too as long as they're happy.

I have percussion colleagues, usually - but not exclusively - the younger ones, who are obsessed with being able to name the individual players in the percussion sections of every orchestra in Britain, in the same way others could name every player in every football team of the English Premiership, and I also know that this practice isn't confined solely to percussion.

Personally, I've never been interested in that, and even now, the only reason that I know who plays where is because I've actually met the player in person. For example, I know the guys in the sections of the Halle Orchestra, Ulster Orchestra and others because I've either worked there or been on trial with them in the past - all great folk too, I may add - but I've literally no idea who the section is in some of the other orchestras.

It doesn't mean that I'm not interested, only that it's not a priority for me to know the names of every percussionist in every orchestra and their preferred brand of sticks. When I was a student and someone would start talking of a random percussion section as though they knew them intimately, I would immediately glaze over and tend to say things along the lines of "Have you ever thought of getting a proper life, or maybe a girlfriend/boyfriend or just some sort of hobby?" which to me now sounds a bit condescending but was really only intended at the time to let the recipient know that I just wasn't that interested.

With time, of course I realised that that was their hobby, and they were absolutely entitled to wax lyrical about it, whether I found it tedious or not, in the same way in which I wax lyrical about my interests here, although at least you can turn the page if you get bored.

It's the equivalent of a young percussion student somewhere who's telling his mates, whether they want to hear it or not, "Yeah, the SBO section is Martin Willis and Owen Williams. Willis has used the same pair of 'Vic Firth SD1 General' snare drum sticks for the last twenty years, and once found a kebab in one of his concert shoes just before a matinee, and Williams likes the odd shot of coffee Patrón of an evening, after a long session at the gym. Yeah, great blokes!"

"Really? Have you ever met them?"

"No."

As far as the importance of music goes, there are still a few conductors who take it to the extreme and will go into an almost apoplectic rage because one note out of sixty-four in a four-bar phrase was played *legato* and not *staccato*.

Maybe it's an age thing, but I've started saying "First World problem, mate" when these precious charlatans start with their tantrums. Yes, we know that you only want it to be the best it can be, just as we - the players - do, but don't be a spoilt child about it.

Mid-way through a tour of Germany and Austria a few years ago, the orchestra had reached the beautiful Alpine city of Innsbruck. Having tuned, we were sitting on stage as the conductor entered and walked through the violins to his rostrum to begin the rehearsal in the new (to us) venue.

"Ladies and gentlemen," he said with a welcoming smile. "Thank you for a truly exceptional concert last night in Wiesbaden. As you know, I don't usually single out people or sections for praise, as it's a team effort but I have to say - trumpets, the last movement of the Tchaikovsky was simply staggering, so bravo." The three trumpets gave a little smile of thanks to the conductor, acknowledging the compliment. "Likewise, the whole woodwind section. You all deserve a mention for your exquisite playing in the concerto - I know the soloist was very pleased indeed". Just as the trumpets had done, the wind all smiled and nodded a small "thanks" back in acknowledgement.

The great maestro turned to the first violin section and smiled. "First violins...", he said. They all smiled back in anticipation of the imminent compliment. "The opening of the Beethoven was unacceptable!"

What?!

"Everyone else leave the stage now. I want fifteen minutes alone with the firsts."

Now, that did not strike me as a spontaneous or off-the-cuff comment, but rather something that had been thought out and well-planned in advance, and which came across as nothing more than petty, vindictive, a crass abuse of power and above all unnecessary.

The only positive thing that came out of that incident was that, on the coach to Munich the next day, the first violins bore the brunt of everyone else's humorous comments and became forever jokingly referred to by their friends and colleagues as either 'The Innsbruck Fourteen' or 'The Unacceptables', in reference to the recently released Stallone/Schwarzenegger movie, 'The Expendables', and both nicknames were worn as a pseudo badge of honour by all of the first violins who were there.

As professional musicians, we all dedicate a large portion of our existence to music and trying to improve ourselves and our playing so that;

1. The music, and our performance of it, is the absolute best it can be and the audience, large or small are left satisfied and not ruing time wasted listening to and/or being insulted by inferior playing.
2. Mainly, we don't look like a total idiot in front of our colleagues

....so, we're not totally oblivious in the strive for perfection.

If there is a mistake by a player, it's almost always a totally genuine one and the thing to remember most is that nobody died because of it.

Obviously, I'm not suggesting that we take our profession less seriously, or that every single musician in the world shouldn't be obsessed with music, as that view would be completely ridiculous.

If most of the orchestral players and world-class soloists with whom we work hadn't been as obsessed as they were about their instrument, there would be a lot less players of quality in general, let alone world-class soloists, and if there were any at all, the bar would really be set pretty low.

I am still obsessed by music, both orchestral and non-orchestral, but just not to the exclusion of everything else, and I believe there are many things that are just as important that will actually complement what we do.

Even so, having interests outwith the world of music, or even if it's only outside of the orchestral genre, I've found to be healthy and can only help to make one more open-minded and much more rounded as a person. This will have a knock-on effect of actually improving one's mental approach to music, and I believe it can only be a good thing.

At the very least it provides a break from orchestral music and the intense cauldron we inhabit there, after which one can return to it, fresh again and with just as much passion.

Having other interests won't make you less dedicated to music, and one shouldn't feel like they're cheating on a long-term partner by doing so, as I know that's how some colleagues feel. Non-music interests will almost exclusively be an enriching experience, so if there are any budding musicians reading this, give it a go if you haven't already - it'll be so worth it and you'll notice the difference in your approach to your playing and outlook towards music in general.

I know professional players who, in their spare time are into lots of varied hobbies and sports which have nothing at all, or very little to do with music.

I have friends and colleagues who are involved in a plethora of interests ranging from Tango dancing, mountaineering in the Alps, *properly* brewing beer, training for a pilot's licence, sailing, train-spotting, plane-spotting, computer coding, cooking to the level of appearing on television's "Masterchef" (as did RSNO 'cellist

Kennedy Leitch), having a pen-pal on Death Row in America – the list is endless, and none of these musicians are boring!

Apart from the train-spotters.

Rik Evans, my pal and violist with the BBC SSO is obsessed not with Mozart or Beethoven, but with AC/DC, the Australian rock mega-group. Specifically, he's obsessed with their rhythm guitarist, Malcolm Young and has even taken numerous guitar lessons to take himself up to the level of being able to play all of Malcolm's parts to an excellent standard. As I write this, I'm the Phil Rudd to his Malcolm in Rik's AC/DC tribute band, and we're in the process of looking for our first gig.

So, who knows, by the time you read this, we might be on a world tour of dingy rock pubs everywhere if we get time off from our respective orchestras. I'm sure they'd probably agree to it too, even if only to get rid of us for a bit.

Outside of Orchestra-World, I've played in a few rock bands for fun. I've mentioned Ragamuffin already, but the one I spent the most time with was a four-piece Rock and Metal band called Havok Road.

Twelve years, one five-track demo on Soundcloud and numerous videos on YouTube, playing rock covers from the likes of Black Sabbath, Rush, Metallica, Thin Lizzy, Led Zeppelin *et al* was quite enough and I left the band in December 2016, still friends with the other three, Paul, Neil and Andy.

We got our name from our original guitarist, Craig, who drove past a street sign on his way to work every day, which read 'Havoc Road' and he'd thought *"That would be a great name for a band!"*

So, Havoc Road was born.

I later changed the spelling to "Havok" as a nod to my favourite physics engine used in video and computer games, the Havok engine.

And I'll repeat now exactly what I said at one of our gigs once, admittedly to a mixed response - about half of the audience got the irony, with the other half just looking bemused - "I bet some of you people don't even HAVE a favourite physics engine..."

We'd played a few times in various low-key venues in the early days, before getting our own headline slot at "Rockers" - next door to the famous "Arches", and a much sought-after gig by every rock band in Glasgow and beyond.

Every city had a monthly publication of a small, double-sided leaflet called the "Gig List", which was distributed free to pubs and clubs and as the name suggests, lists all the bands playing in every venue in the city for that month.

We couldn't wait to see our name in print, headlining - Havok Road live at Rockers! - and I waited with barely concealed excitement for it to be published. Every day, in the last week of the preceding month, I would walk into bars at all times of the day and ask "Is next month's Gig List out yet?", always leaving dejectedly to try again the next day.

Eventually, on the last day of the month I struck lucky and got hold of the list for the coming month. I immediately went to the Rock and Blues section, found the 'Saturdays' column and scanned down it, searching for Rockers.

Then I saw it.

No.... it can't be...!

In big, bold, black letters, to my eternal chagrin and the echoes of monumental hysterical laughter from a multitude of other bands was our headline listing in true Spinal Tap form;

Rockers, 9pm: HADDOCK ROAD

Nice one, whoever mumbled that over the phone to the printers.

Over the years, I've had some non-music interests which I have been really passionate about, and the first big love I had was volleyball. I carried it on from my school days and through my student years at the Academy, mainly playing competitively for Clydebank Volleyball Club.

After that, I was totally absorbed in fencing.

One of the hardest sports, with the most complex set of rules in which I've ever been involved.

Out of the three sporting weapons of Foil, Épée and Sabre, all with different target areas and techniques, I specialised in foil.

My last fencing competition was the Scottish Open Fencing Championships at Meadowbank Sports Centre in Edinburgh in the mid-nineties, where I did well (at least I thought I did) but was eventually 'bested' - and I use that term very loosely indeed - by an ignoble knave of low breeding and ungentlemanly morals.

That may sound a bit like sour grapes, but in truth I was beaten by an inferior fencer who took dastardly advantage of a sly opportunity, with a total disregard and absence of all honour and integrity, the mainstay of this sport.

Before and after each bout, even at weekly training sessions, you must salute your opponent. Not only that, but it must be done properly - mask up to show face, weapon down at the side and pointing downwards before being brought up smartly with the guard at chin level, blade pointing straight up and then smartly back down to its original position again.

I have to confess here - I can't stand a sloppy salute! That just used to make me more determined to beat the perpetrator.

Fencing is the only sport I can think of in which a participant can be black-carded for refusing to salute, resulting in immediate expulsion from the entire competition.

Back at the Scottish Open, I was in a pool of eight fencers, with only the winner going through to the next round.

Of those eight, six were left-handed.

Six! I'd never fenced a left-hander before, ever, and now I had to face six.

Not all at the same time, mind you, just one at a time but that was bad enough.

Anyway, I chatted with the only other right-hander in my pool and he let slip about a technique that he used against lefties.

This basically involved a *feint* to the *quarte* area of the opponent's body, followed by a *counter-disengage* underneath and to the outside of their blade and followed by a thrust in conjunction with either an *attack au fer,* a *lunge* or *flèche* to a small area on their left shoulder, in the *sixte* area. The premise of this was that it was such a small target area that they wouldn't be expecting it, and also wouldn't be totally comfortable defending it in the first place.

Incidentally, don't worry if you're a bit confused with all this.

I was often confused at training sessions with the amount of terminology and rules flying around. There's a small glossary at the back of this book, of the terms I've used, but it's worth checking out Wikipedia, and/or *britishfencing.com* for the full glossary.

Anyway, this pseudo-trickery seemed to work, and it eventually came down to the last bout, which was between me and one of the southpaws.

It was all even between us and down to the last point. Whoever wins this point will go through to the next round.

I hadn't used my secret technique against this opponent yet, so I decided that now was the time.

In fencing, if there is a tied point, i.e. if both parties hit each other simultaneously, then the fencer who is advancing, or started their attack first - known as 'having right of way' - will be awarded the point.

On the command "*Allez!*" ("*Go!*") from the referee, I immediately advanced towards my opponent, thereby giving myself an early advantage.

I already knew in my head what my general tactics would be for this final point, and although he appeared to be a decent fencer, I was confident that my final thrust would be too quick for him, even if he spotted it coming.

This point is indelibly printed in my memory as, to this day, I still can't believe what he did.

I advanced with my foil arm extended, until I reached a point where - judging by his reach - if we both lunged at the same time, would be where the tips of our respective weapons would meet, with no danger of either of us scoring against the other.

Just as I got there, I used one of my favourite *phrases* that I normally used against right-handers, or "normal people" as I like to call them.

I quickly withdrew my arm, hoping to confuse his judgment of my reach and immediately *lunged* with an *attack au fer* before a rapid back-foot recovery into a split-second *en guard* position followed by a *balestra* and another *lunge* to cover a lot of ground quickly and take me within scoring distance.

It probably sounds a bit convoluted, but in reality, it's actually all pretty basic moves and easy enough to adapt when the opponent invariably doesn't do what I was hoping they would.

As I *lunged* for the final time, I started a thrust at his *sixte* area, and as he went for the expected *parry*, I *disengaged* under his blade, still moving forward mid-*lunge,* and went for the final, lightning thrust against his upper *quarte.*

Now, I'm convinced that what happened next was a total fluke and he just threw his arm to the side in panic.

Whatever, though, it worked.

An analysis of this *phrase* would, without doubt, say that as I *disengaged,* and my blade passed under his, on its way up to his shoulder, he *counter-parried* and hit my weapon with such force - or maybe only by good fortune - and connected with it on a weakened spot along its length and at the beginning of its *foible,* that my blade broke in half.

What the...?! My blade!

I stood there motionless as I heard a muffled 'clang' through my mask, the sound of the broken portion of my blade hitting the floor, and felt my weapon instantaneously lose all its weight, and even with its 'orthopaedic' pistol-grip, it now felt like I was holding a feather in my right hand.

I stared in disbelief at what was left of my foil, looked up from my broken sword and straight at my opponent.

He was standing with his weapon at his side, and although I couldn't see his face through his mask, by his stance he appeared to be just as surprised as I was.

Time now seemed to go in slow motion, and before the referee could call a time out for a weapon change, my opponent very slowly lifted his foil and ever so gently touched me, right in the middle of my chest, as I stood there, now unarmed and helpless.

The buzzer went off with a coloured light denoting a hit on target.

The dastardly rapscallion!... as Errol Flynn would have no doubt said, although it wasn't quite the phrase that immediately went through my head.

There were a few "boo's" from some other fencers who were watching our bout, which I appreciated but it didn't change anything and there was nothing I could do about it.

It's not against the rules, but it's absolutely frowned upon and I was livid!

Fencing has a very strong element of honour, chivalry and sportsmanship running through it, and that was none of them.

He lifted his mask, now the winner and without looking me in the eye, said "Sorry, we're not supposed to do that!" followed by a little nervous laugh. "Hehe..."
He went through to the next round, I went out.
Not that I'm bitter about it or anything....

After that, my ardour for fencing died away quite a bit, and although not completely, I found something else that I became as equally excited about as I had been about fencing, and it probably couldn't be any further removed from music.

Chapter Fifteen

Blue Skies

As summer 2007 approached, I suddenly realised that for the previous couple of years, I had been in need of a challenge. I reckon it was the programming - by all of the orchestras - that had, purely by coincidence, all converged into one huge "easy play" for me personally, with the only challenge being to get through most of the concerts without falling asleep. They were mostly full of mainly popular pieces that I had played a million times before and could, sadly, get by a bit on autopilot.

It had also definitely been quite a few years since I'd come off stage with any sort of a 'buzz' after an orchestral concert.

There had been a few really enjoyable tours in these couple of years to break the monotony - Spain, South America and a couple of others - but by and large, I was bored and came to the conclusion that I needed a challenge of some sort.

Something I had always wanted to do ever since I was a kid had been making a resurgence in my brain for the past few years, and I'd been thinking about it more and more. I decided that as I was now forty-one, if I didn't do something about it now, I'd never do it at all.

So, in April 2007, after doing a lot of research online, I booked myself onto a course at Strathallan airfield near Perth, on the 8th June that year for my first solo parachute jump.

At the time of writing this, I've done a total of three jumps, or a "massive" total of three jumps, as I like to make ironically clear. People have said "Well, it's three more than I've done", but if you think that most of the instructors at Strathallan have literally hundreds or even thousands of jumps under their belts, it puts it into perspective a bit.

Having gone to bed early on the Friday evening and after a night restless with nervous excitement and anticipation, I got up early and set off just after 7.00am for the hour's drive to the airfield.

Even at that time in the morning, when I arrived just after 8.00am, the place was packed and really busy with lots of people milling about, waiting to be told where to go.

A couple of instructors - a male and a female - appeared and the female announced "All those who are here for a tandem jump, follow Steve here into that room over there and he'll get you sorted out", pointing at a doorway leading into an adjacent room. "Everyone for the Static Line course, follow me up the stairs".

That was me.

I followed six others and the instructor up the stairs and into a small, brightly-lit classroom with a couple of large tables conjoined to make one big enough for us all to sit around.

The instructor's name was Joyce, and when we had all completed filling in various forms and paid the remaining balance for the course, we got down to business.

After being shown where everything was via an "orientation of the Drop-Zone" session, which featured the highlight of being taken to "The Gravel Pit" and told to avoid landing in it at all costs, we headed back to the classroom.

One of the other students asked Joyce "So, how dangerous is skydiving really?" with just a hint of trepidation and looking for a small reassurance that things would be ok.

The Scottish Parachute Club run these courses every weekend, and the instructors have to answer this question more than any other, and they take pride in seeing the effect that the answer, in their twisted skydive humour, has on the students.

"Well, statistically you've got more chance of winning the National Lottery than you have of something going wrong with your jump today".

We all breathed an audible sigh of relief, which turned out to be very short-lived when she continued.

"However," said Joyce, with a mischievous glint in her eye, "every week, someone wins the lottery, and if they don't, it's a roll-over".

We were bombarded with an enormous amount of information and covered everything theoretical, from the mechanics of the canopy (how the thing actually works and flies), canopy control, hazard recognition and impact procedure, to all the in-air safety checks post-exit and implementing a flight plan.

Between that and all the physical training, including practicing our arched/spread positions, landing properly from a little three-foot high platform, exit procedure from the mock-up Cessna in the hangar, malfunction procedure, suspended harness drills and a few walkthroughs of our flight plan, we were ready to jump.

Unfortunately, the wind was too strong for any jumping that day, and I was forced to drive back home, disappointed, but with the intention of returning the next day.

I awoke on the Sunday, around 7:30am and thought how easy it would be to stay in bed and tell myself "It's fine, I'll go next weekend", and basically talk myself out of it. I got straight out of bed and got ready to go back to Strathallan, because I knew that if I did stay at home that day, then the moment would have gone and I would never do it.

After hanging about at the airfield and staring at a windsock for hours on end, waiting for the wind to subside, I eventually jumped around 4pm, and it was the second-most scariest thing I've ever done in my life.

It was also the best.

Adrenaline-fuelled, I never slept at all for the following two nights, and barely slept for the next three after that.

A few people I knew who had experience with skydiving (including Allan Hannah whose total was almost one hundred jumps from his Army days) had all told me "Do your second jump straight away. Don't leave it - do it immediately!"

So, following their advice to the letter, and eight years later, in the first week of April 2015, I stopped in the street on the way from my hotel to a SB matinee of "A Streetcar Named Desire" at Sadlers Wells Theatre in London and booked my second jump, for Saturday 6th June - the scariest thing I've ever done, because I now knew what it was actually like.

June 6th arrived, and I repeated the same course I'd done eight years previously. I was pretty certain that I had remembered everything from the first time, but it soon became apparent that I'd actually forgotten more than I'd remembered.

This time, there were five of us on the course.

Myself, an 18-year-old nice, bubbly girl whose mother waited all day in the car park for her to finish, two Polish guys aged 31 and 39 who worked at a potato factory just outside Glasgow, and a lovely late-twenty's Brazilian girl called Zaira, who would later become one of my jump partners. She had used public transport to get to Strathallan Airfield and had left Glasgow at 5am to reach the airfield in time.

As it turned out, all jumping was cancelled that day, once again due to the high wind, and as I would be going past Zaira's house anyway, I offered her a lift home.

On the way home, we discussed everything that we'd been taught that day and she decided to definitely come back with me the next day to hopefully jump, but we'd obviously have to wait and see what tomorrow's weather would be like before going back up to Perthshire.

As the early morning turned out to be nice, but still windy, I picked her up again and we headed back to the airfield, once again talking about the course.

One thing that Zaira said was "What was the situation that involves pulling only one cord and not the whole bunch that comes out of the riser?" (*The **riser** is the strap-like length of material attached to the harness at the shoulders, out of which emanates all the lines connected to the canopy*).

I said that I thought that was for when we'd landed and the canopy was still fully developed, so it would be pulling you along the ground, just choose any single cord and pull it, and one end of the canopy would collapse and problem solved. Then, because we'd been bombarded with so much information the day before, I started to doubt that myself, but there is a reason why I've mentioned this, which I'll get to later.

When we arrived, we went straight to "manifest", the organisational room of the whole drop zone (DZ), where the person in charge has to deal with everyone who wants to jump, putting their names on one of four different boards. They have to organise lifts (aeroplane trips up to a specific altitude) into static line, tandem or free fall - the experience, weight, etc., of each individual person... quite a monumental task, I thought. The day before, when we'd been shown where everything was, Sergei, our mental Russian instructor said, in his thick accent "If you want to know what the weather is going to be like for the rest of the day, don't annoy person in charge of manifest - we have a special machine for that". He then pointed to a large novelty crystal ball on the main counter. "Don't ask stupid questions", and walked away, chuckling to himself.

While taking us through the rig store, where we would collect the packs containing our parachutes when the time came to jump, he also said with a massive grin "Make sure you take your packs from this side on the left, marked "Static Line" and not from the ones on the right-hand side, marked "Freefall". Otherwise you get big surprise!"

They put out a call for an instructor to do a 'refresher' for a couple of first-time students (I was classed as a first timer because my first jump was 8 years ago), and a really nice chap called Callum arrived, told us to collect and put on jump suits, training harnesses and helmets, and meet him at the mock-up plane in the hangar. He then took us through exit procedure a few times each, randomly throwing in a "malfunction!" to get us to do our malfunction procedure.

The exit procedure goes as follows:

Sitting as far out of the open door of the plane as possible, facing forward in the direction of travel, legs out and knees slightly bent, head looking up and in towards the pilot's head, on the command "GO", push off hard with the left hand and land on the mat - without looking at it - then shout your count.

The count differs depending on the length of freefall, and for us it was a five-second count.

As soon as you exit the plane, the first thing you shout is "Arch!" as an aid to help you to remember to arch your back for stability in the air, and "thousand" helps to fill out each second, to prevent counting too quickly. If the count is too fast, there's a possibility that a canopy which is still in the process of opening could be mistaken for a malfunction, and the student would then cut away a perfectly good parachute unnecessarily.

"ARCH THOUSAND

TWO THOUSAND
THREE THOUSAND
FOUR THOUSAND
CHECK CANOPY!"

The instructor might then shout "Malfunction!" and the student then shouts the malfunction procedure:

"LOOK
CUT
AWAY
RESERVE
ARCH!"

LOOK - *look for the small rectangular cutaway pad - which is attached to the lines running through the harness and connected to the main canopy by a series of rings - located on the front right-hand side of the harness, and grab it with the right hand, left hand on top.*
　CUT - *tear the pad upwards along the length of its Velcro edge until it's no longer attached to the harness.*
　AWAY - *still holding the pad, thrust both arms downward which will release the main canopy and you will enter freefall - then drop the pad.*
　RESERVE - *locate the silver reserve canopy handle, situated on the front left-hand side of the harness, insert left hand thumb and grab it, right hand on top and push it away from your body, releasing the reserve parachute.*
　ARCH - *arch your back for stability again.*

And it's as easy as that.

Obviously, I'm being flippant and it's not easy at all, especially in a high stress situation, hence the reason it has to be practiced repeatedly until you can do it in your sleep.
　The first time Callum chucked in a "malfunction", it was my turn to exit, and not expecting it I got a bit of a shock. And this was on the ground! What would it be like if it was for real, in mid-air at 70-plus mph and accelerating?

I tried hard not to think too much about it and did a few more exits/malfunctions. I got a "Nailed it, mate - you were all over it!" from Callum, so I was pleased and ready to cope with anything now.

The pair of us then went back to manifest and put our names on the board for first-time students.

I was told to put "BB" beside my name, as I was over 12 stones in weight.

I'm sure I don't need to explain that one...

Now all we could do was to wait until we were called.

We'd arrived about 11.15 am and it was now almost noon. The sun was shining, with lovely blue skies and a few decent sized clouds but they were pretty high up, even to my untrained eye and well above our 3,500 feet jump height.

The next eight hours though, can really be summed up in five words - staring at a windsock again.

Zaira and I spent this time in either the quiet lounge or the café area, which was pretty noisy and busy with quite a lot of experienced parachutists, tandem jumpers, students more experienced than us two, and all their families here for a day out to watch the skydiving.

Occasionally, the P.A. system would give a little crackle before an announcement, which for the first couple of hours was always "Attention all at the drop zone - wind is still too strong for any jumps, we'll keep you informed". These announcements happened about every 15 to 20 minutes, and after about 3 or 4 announcements, when we heard the little crackle, we both got a touch of the butterflies.

Around 1.30pm, the announcement suddenly changed to "Wind safe for a two hundred limit", i.e. it was now safe enough for those with a total of 200 or more jumps.

So we sat and waited, talked a lot, had a few long but strangely not awkward silences as we each thought our own things over. Neither of us ate anything at all - for some reason we weren't all that hungry...

We went outside for a bit to watch the big boys and girls take off, go up to ten thousand feet, where the plane was a tiny speck against the blue sky and watched them freefall until their canopies deployed and they came down fast, sometimes racing each other, which I'm sure they'll all deny that that's what they were doing.

If you've ever seen the movie "Monsters Inc.", when the big, cool monsters come out in slow motion to start their work and the little janitor/cleaner monster says in admiration "They're so awesome!" you'll get an idea of how I was feeling at that moment.

Zaira and myself discussed the option of setting a time limit to leave the DZ and go back home and to try again next weekend, as the wind, now gusting between 1-2mph immediately to 17-18mph was still a problem, but we both decided to stick it out as it was now around 5pm and some of the guys had told us that it had all the signs of calming down in the early evening.

As the day wore on, the people jumped and then left with their families and the DZ started to become pretty quiet, but more importantly, the wind was beginning to settle. Manifest told us "We're sending up an experienced student who's doing a 10 second delay (freefall) and we'll see what she says".

This got our hopes up, and we went outside to watch American Lauren do her 21st jump - 4 away from getting her A-Licence to allow her to jump on her own at maximum altitude anywhere in the world.

About 15 minutes after she touched down and had had her de-briefing, I was in the café area with Zaira when I saw Joyce, the instructor who had jumped with Lauren, approach the only two other students left, apart from us, speak quickly to them outside, then I heard her say "Where's the other two?".

This could be it.

It was now about 8.30pm and she was either going to tell us to go home, or we were going to jump right now.

She appeared through the door and said "You two - get kitted up! I'll be your dispatcher" and left through the door that led to the hangar area.

The four of us followed her quickly through the door and immediately put on our jump suits.

These, incidentally only come in two sizes - either too big or too small. We both then had to take them off again because we'd forgotten to put on our buoyancy aids, small life-vests around our necks, and possibly quite vital if we landed in the River Earn, which runs along one side of the airfield.

Jump suits back on, we each collected our own helmet, radio and altimeter and went back to the student kit-up area where, to save time, our packs were already waiting for us, courtesy of Alwyn, a young, very experienced parachutist, who'd actually first demonstrated the malfunction procedure to our class yesterday.

She laid out my pack and held it as I stepped into the leg straps, then lifted it up for me to put my arms through. I adjusted the leg straps, pulling them tight, so that there would be no movement there when I was in the air. I later discovered I'd pulled them a bit too tight and ended up with a big red scrape in a place that, as much as I would have liked to, I couldn't really show anyone. Anyway, I didn't discover that until after I'd landed, so it was all fine for the moment.

We then threaded our chest-straps through our altimeters and let them hang a little bit. We were assured they'd pop up into position when we exited, and I remembered that from the last time, so I really didn't think twice that it was on my chest and pointing away from me so I couldn't see it, as I'd be able to see it fine later, when I really needed to.

Now Joyce walked outside the hanger area, about 50 feet away and tested our helmet radios. "Raise your right hand if you can hear me". Three of us raised our right hands and Alex, a student at Strathclyde University on this, his third jump, raised his left hand. "Right hand!" came back through the radio and he quickly realised his mistake and raised his right. Joyce came back in and walked up to Alex, adjusted one of his straps and said "You're going to die if you do stupid things like that". This was said not in a way to belittle him, but to impress on all of us the enormity and seriousness of what we were about to do and to focus us on everything we'd learned so far.

It certainly worked for me, I can tell you.

The final thing we needed to do was look at our flight plan, so we gathered around a large aerial photograph of the airfield, hanging on the wall and Joyce told us "I've just been up, so we don't need to throw out a wind indicator for this one. The wind is moving in this direction, so you'll be dropped off here," and she pointed to an area just east of the airfield.

"You'll start your flight plan at 1,500 feet here", indicating the north-east corner of the rectangular runway, "and run with wind (wind from behind) in a straight line to here (north-west corner) and between 800-500 feet turn and fly cross wind until you're here at the south-west corner and at 300 feet start your final holding (into wind) approach and land. Everyone clear?"

Yes, we were all clear.

Next, she numbered us 1 to 4. Number 4 was a student who was doing her ninth jump with a 5-second delay. As she'd be dropping from a higher altitude than the three of us, and therefore be the last one out, she would board the aircraft first. The order is then based on weight, and Zaira, at a petite 5'2" and slightly built was number 3. I was designated number 1 - last in, first out.

First out?! I decided then and there that if I landed in one piece, I was definitely going on a diet...

Our static lines were then released from our pack by Joyce, the hook opened and put in our left hand, not to be let go of until we hooked on in the plane.

Joyce said "Right, let's go" and we followed her in order, me bringing up the rear, to the holding pen (a small fenced-off area, where only parachutists are allowed in) and a short wait for the little white Cessna 206 to arrive for us. It pulled up right at the exit of the holding pen and switched off its engine. As we approached it from the rear, I remember Sergei telling us yesterday "Always approach aircraft from side or rear - not from front. That's where propeller is and it will definitely ruin your make-up". I found the guy incredibly likeable and very funny.

Last in, I turned and sat on the edge of the doorway and handed my static line back to Joyce who hooked it onto the wire running along the floor and almost against the opposite side of the fuselage.

"Check your line. Is it secure?"

I gave it three robust tugs and said "Yes".

When we exit shortly, the other end of the static line, i.e. the end attached to us, will open the pack and pull out a bag containing the parachute which will (hopefully) automatically deploy itself in the fast-flowing air.

We were all now inside the aircraft.

Number 4 was on the floor beside the pilot's seat, and the only one of us facing forward, Zaira, number 3, sat with her pack against the back of the pilot's seat. Number two sat beside her, his pack against number 4's, and I was beside him, my pack squeezed right up against Zaira's front.

Our dispatcher then climbed in and adopted a kneeling-on-one-leg position, blocking the doorway for the other three but not me. I could feel her grab the back of my pack with her left hand and hold me as securely as she could, as she steadied herself by taking hold of a small handle just above the doorway with her right hand.

She then said to the pilot "Right, Chris. Three runs at three and a half (thousand feet) and one at four".

"Righto, Joyce!" came the cheery reply.

I thought *"How can you be so cheery at a time like this, Chris, you cheery sod?!"*

The engine started and we slowly moved forward, turned 180 degrees and started taxing to the end of the runway. The small Cessna turned again, eastwards into the wind, immediately sped up and was off the ground in a few seconds.

Now, the wind which had very kindly died down for us, suddenly changed its mind and started gusting as soon as we left the ground and although Cheery Chris was coping admirably, we were getting thrown around quite a bit. Even though we could hardly hear someone shouting over the noise of the engine, I'm sure I could hear him whistling the theme tune to "Those Magnificent Men In Their Flying Machines".

We've all been in planes and experienced turbulence, but sitting on the floor of a small plane, with no seatbelt, travelling backwards, arms crossed and covering your handles (main canopy cutaway pad and reserve handle), next to an open door with nothing between you and it, as the massive aircraft hangar below gets smaller and smaller really quickly, in turbulence, is definitely one of the best laxatives known to man.

I looked out the door a couple of times at the trees and fields rapidly shrinking, and decided to stare straight ahead at my feet, which were pushing against the edge of a little wooden strut almost in the tail area and was my only point of support of any kind, and not turn my head again until I had to. I noticed at that point my breathing was quite fast and shallow, so I took some deliberate slow, deep breaths for about 30 seconds and that worked well, just like Sergei told us.

Getting close to altitude, Joyce reached over, flipped my altimeter up to check it was working, let it drop again and gave me the thumbs up.

Great! At least I know that's working!

Feeling more movement behind me, and a push to make me lean forward, I did just that and Joyce squeezed past and manoeuvred into position at my feet until she was face-to-face with me.

She pointed to my left foot and then indicated for me to move it to the other side of her, then the same with my right foot. If I were to move my left foot two inches more to the left now, it would be out the door.

She looked up at the pilot and shouted "Cut!"

Chris cut the engine and we were now travelling at a leisurely 70-80 mph.

She then looked at me, and without the slightest bit of pity shouted "Number One, feet out!"

I shuffled into exit position, dropped my feet out the door and immediately felt the strength of the wind try to tear my legs away. I stuck my right arm straight out behind me, holding the doorway to prevent my pack hitting it on the way out, left hand on the edge of the fuselage floor, thumb on the outside of the aircraft, and tried to sit as far out as I physically could, leaning forward in the direction of travel. It takes a lot of effort to actually get out, as the fast-flowing air outside is forcing you back inside the aircraft. A couple of big efforts and I was as far out as I could go, just barely sitting on the edge, looking down and in a bit at the floor and - with a knot in my stomach - knowing what was coming next.

"Head up!"

I lifted my head and looked up at the back of the pilot's head and immediately heard "GO!"

Without hesitation (phew!) I kicked my legs out, like you'd do on a swing for momentum, and pushed off with my left hand as hard as I could, arched my back, stretched out my arms and legs to make myself as big as possible and started my count.

Then I don't know what happened.

It felt like I'd been flipped somehow.

My count instantly disappeared, and I suddenly felt a MASSIVE rapid deceleration like being suddenly and violently dragged backward from a standing position by a race car, and it took all the air out of my lungs with a massive "OOOF!"

I found out at the debriefing later that I had turned 90 degrees on exit, turned either by the wind or, more likely, a less than perfect exit.

The time from exit to canopy deployment seemed to be really fast, much quicker than my first time, and once I realised it was open, I knew I had to check it and worry about my exit after I'd done that.

Ok, canopy check - is it big, rectangular and does it look controllable?

"Yes" to all three - no malfunction!

Yippee!

I then took a few seconds to try to work out what the hell had happened on my exit, couldn't fathom it at all, so I tried to put it straight out of my mind and started my safety checks, top to bottom.

1. Release brakes - *I looked up and located the two yellow steering toggles and pulled them out of their Velcro fastenings.*

2. Pump toggles all the way down three times and check canopy again for end-cell collapse - *One, two, three, look up and check*...all fine!

3. Segregation check - *Look around for other parachutes in close proximity*...no-one here, just me.

4. Control check - *look left, steer left, same again right, then test flare, both toggles down all the way*...all working fine.

5. System check - *check reserve handle and yellow cut away pad are still visible and properly attached*...yep, they're still there ok.

Checks done - all fine.

Now to enjoy flying about for a bit until I reach 1,500 feet when I need to be in position to start my flight plan. I checked my altimeter. It hadn't popped up!

It was still facing away from me and I couldn't read it, and that meant I had no idea how high I was.

I have to land facing into the wind, hence the flight plan, but if I have no idea of my altitude, I could easily overshoot the landing zone and end up anywhere.

I tried to think of our hazard recognition class, which dealt with impacting on things like trees, houses, electric pylons and landing on a busy road or in a river.

Unfortunately, the only thing I could remember about it was the instructor saying "A cow will stand and watch you fly into it".

Nothing else.

I just knew I was going to hit a cow!

Afterwards, a few people asked "Why didn't you just reach down to your altimeter with your hand and tilt it up?"

"Two reasons," was my reply to them.

"Firstly, it never even entered my mind, which was just about coping with the sensory overload of my woefully bad exit, and secondly, because of the first reason, there was nothing on this Earth that would make either of my hands let go of the steering toggles at that particular moment."

So, that's them told.

Just then, from the radio on the left side of my helmet came the voice of an angel - a big burly angel called Ciaran, with over seven thousand jumps, but a calm-voiced, ground communication angel to me, nonetheless.

"Number One, pull your left toggle all the way down if you can hear me."

I pulled it all the way down.

"Same with your right toggle."

I did that too.

"That's good. Ok, you're out of position. Pull left...left...left..."

This went on for the next few minutes as Ciaran guided me down and into a position where I was facing the correct way for landing. I could see the ground below moving quite fast as I got closer to it - faster than I remembered it from the last time.

"Number One, legs together in landing position and ready to flare in three... two... one...flare!"

I pulled both toggles all the way down as far as I could and held them there, and I went from moving at around 20mph to completely stationary and I dropped straight downwards, all the while hearing a calmly but firmly spoken "Hold...hold...hold..." in my radio.

Suddenly, I felt the canopy – and myself - being blown backwards by the strong wind as I dropped, but I held the toggles where they were.

This was the most critical point of the landing procedure which had been impressed on us many times during training.

If I released the tension on the toggles now, the canopy would lurch forward and it would be highly likely that I'd be smashed into the ground at speed which, if I'm honest, wouldn't really be my ideal choice for a method of landing.

This aside, though, I was still determined to land on my feet....and I did!

A split-second later, the wind fully caught the canopy, which then became a very large and powerful kite, and it immediately dragged me straight onto my back with another undignified "OOOF!"

I scrambled to my feet and pulled one of my risers to try to control the canopy which was blowing and spinning wildly around, but the force of it was so immense that it pulled me over for a second time.

That's when I remembered the conversation with Zaira earlier that day, and so, from a half-kneeling position, I grabbed a single cord at random, gave it a good hard pull and the whole canopy collapsed and died immediately.

I stood up and walked towards it, coiling the lines as I went and gathered up the parachute itself, made my way back to the DZ and waited for the others to land, which they all did safely, thankfully.

As we were told the previous day by Sergei, "This is sport parachuting and you're not in the military, so no-one will force you to jump.

The only time that will happen is if you're in the plane and you hear "Emergency! Exit, exit, exit!" If you hear that, exit the plane immediately, in usual order. If you're taking too long, you will be 'assisted'.

In a normal situation if you hesitate at the door and don't want to jump, it's not a problem. We'll bring the aircraft back down, drop you off and head back up to jump height for any others left inside."

In 2016/2017 season, there were just under six and a half thousand full-time members of the British Parachute Association, so it is a fairly unusual and niche sport in which to participate, although the numbers are steadily rising, which I think is great.

There are two reasons why I've only done three jumps – time and weather.

Most parachute/skydiving clubs in the UK are only open at weekends, and Strathallan is one of them, only opening on Saturdays and Sundays, when musicians are normally working. On the few occasions when I did have the weekend off, I would do the hour's drive, and a quick refresher from the mock-up (compulsory for students before being allowed to jump) only to find that the Scottish weather had put paid to any jumping whatsoever, whether because of the wind, rain, low cloud, or once, actual sleet out of nowhere. If one wants to progress in the sport, one invariably has to go abroad, usually to Spain, where the weather is more or less guaranteed to be skydiving-friendly.

As such, I only know of two other professional orchestral musicians who have been involved in skydiving.

Steve Cowling, Principal Horn in the SBO and one of the funniest people I know, has done two static-line jumps and, like me, would love to go abroad for an intensive course, but work commitments have forced him to put it on hold for the moment.

The other professional orchestral musician is Ralph Tartaglia, a violist with the Ulster Orchestra.

Steve has done two static-lines.

I've done three static-lines.

Ralph has done seven hundred and ninety-one freefall jumps and is a qualified aerial cameraman.

Even although I'd only met Ralph a few times before when I'd been working with the UO, I had always been impressed by the stories about him, told to me by other people, and after I'd done my first jump, he became more of an inspiration, albeit from a distance, as it were, because I was always pretty sure that Ralph probably wouldn't have remembered even meeting me as it was only briefly.

I had always intended to include Ralph in this, so after I'd managed to get hold of his contact details, I phoned him up and introduced myself, quickly following up with "This is probably going to be the weirdest phone call you get all day".

Ralph laughed and was immediately the most helpful, open and amenable person ever, as we chatted about his skydiving history and exploits and how it impacted on his professional life.

Even though I'd done so pitifully few jumps in comparison, I found that I could actually relate to quite a fair bit of what Ralph said.

He joined the Ulster Orchestra in October 1990 after freelancing in Manchester and Italy.

"It was the following summer, when I went on holiday with two friends, that one of them asked me if I fancied doing a parachute jump for charity, as he had done two static line jumps (on round, uncontrollable canopies) 2 years previously and fancied doing another as the 'chutes were now square (and now controllable).

Obviously, I said yes. I've always been a bit of an adrenalin seeker!

We ended up jumping in September 1991 and as soon as we landed, my friend and I signed up for the course.

To date, I have 791 jumps, mostly camera jumps, as that is what I'd always wanted to do.

I achieved my category 8 (allowing the parachutist to jump from maximum height, on their own anywhere in the world), then category 10 (the final category for advanced skydiving) all at the Wildgeese Skydive Centre, Northern Ireland, and I achieved my Freefly 1 with the Babylon Freefly team in Empuriabrava, Spain in 2002.

Finding time to skydive is always difficult when you have a job. You have to rely on free time at weekends, weather permitting or go abroad for a week of intense jumping. This got more difficult as the kids came along - 3 of them! Anytime I had I would go up to the DZ regardless of the weather. It's the only way in this country if you want to jump. It takes over your life!"

I asked Ralph if skydiving has had any positive or negative effects on his playing or professional life.

"One way in which it helped my playing was that it gave me a complete break from music. When you arrive at a DZ, all you talk about is skydiving with people from all walks of life. Work is never mentioned. Then, preparing for each jump, you have to clear your mind and focus. There is nothing better than jumping out of a plane at 13,000ft to completely de-stress! No-one who hasn't jumped can ever understand the freedom of mind when you leave the plane. I always went back to work, still buzzing from jumping and much more relaxed.

The only "negative" about skydiving has been the switch in passion for my sport instead of music. I would rather be skydiving than playing the viola!"

I also asked Ralph how many other professional orchestral players he knew, who were involved in skydiving, and his answer was rather surprising.

"You are the only other musician that I've met who has jumped!"

I then more or less forced him to detail some of his exploits, and so here comes more inspiration...

"As regards my exploits, I've jumped in Gap France before I got my category 8.

I went to Skydive Deland in Florida with a 4-way team as cameraman, to get coaching for the up and coming British Nationals at Skydive Hibaldstow in 2003. We were coached by a member of the then world 4-way champions, Deland Magic, in the air and in the wind tunnel.

Then I competed in the Nationals that summer in the junior 4-way competition which was an unbelievable experience. I had top cameramen helping me with my camera work.

I went 3 times to Skydive Empuriabrava in Spain, where I learned to Freefly and do some camera jumps.

I've also filmed [*several*] 15-ways at the Wildgeese Centre, joined by the Irish Parachute club! (The word 'way' is used when you jump with others, linking up and creating formations, i.e. 4-way teams, 8-way etc... We had 15 in the sky trying to make certain formations, so one formation all linked up is a 15-way). I've filmed approximately 400 Tandem jumps at the 'Geese."

Now that is definitely awesome!

I certainly haven't given up and have for some time now been eyeing up courses in Empuriabrava, but until then I'd better continue practising my scales, arpeggios and paradiddles.

I love the fact that I am inspired by some musicians, but not because of their musical prowess – even though Ralph is a fantastic viola player! – and that inspiration does seep into all aspects of life, even the orchestral side.

If you've ever thought, even fleetingly, about doing a parachute jump, then go for it. I cannot recommend it highly enough, and it will be the best experience you'll probably ever have.

And Ralph – Blue Skies, sir!

Allan Hannah *(on right)* surrounded by the orchestra, is presented with a gift of thanks by BBC Scotland Controller, **John McCormick**, **China**, 2000.

(below) The "BBC SSO" percussion section backstage, **Guangzhou, China**, 2000. (l-r), **Dave Lyons** (BBC SSO), **Ian Coulter** (SBO), Martin Willis (SBO), **John Poulter** (RSNO).

My Hero. An iconic photo of two Glasgow firemen, mid-rescue. The fireman on the right is **my father, Martin**. I took this photo of his scrap-book cutting from the front page of the now-defunct Glasgow Evening Citizen, hence the vertical fold along the centre. 16 people were rescued at this fire, April 4th, 1973. The headline from the following day's Scottish Daily Express says it all.

Advertising the BBC SSO concert at the famous **Mozarteum, Rosario, Argentina.** The 2006 **South American** tour also included **Brazil** and **Uruguay.**

Inadvertently caught up in street protests, **Buenos Aires, Argentina,** 2006.

Advertising for what would turn out to be our last gig, headlining at **The Bungalow, Paisley**, and not a fish in sight! Photo used with kind permission of Claire McRae.

Havok Road. *(l-r)*, **Andy Burns**, **Paul Allison**, Martin Willis, **Neil Allison**. Photo used with kind permission of Claire McRae.

My first jump, 2007. I'm the white helmet fourth from the left, in middle of picture, following our pilot and dispatcher to the plane.

A total inspiration. **Ralph Tartaglia**, violist with the Ulster Orchestra, in freefall, wearing a white bow tie, evening tails and holding an inflatable trumpet. Awesome.

In comparison, me - just about managing to turn right.

Proms in the Park, **Glasgow Green,** 2016. The "neck bolts" are in-ear monitors about to be used for playing with **KT Tunstall**.

Suddenly I See - *(l-r)* **KT Tunstall**, Martin Willis, **Dave Lyons, Glynn Forrest**.

Chapter Sixteen

Variations On A Theme

For this penultimate chapter, there follows the Top Ten incidents or instances of note that I feel deserve to be included here, all of which are memorable to me, not always for the best reasons, but do deserve to be here on their own merit nonetheless.

All have lodged in my head as isolated highlights over the years, or at least have just stuck out, as I'm sure most of them have also stuck in the memories of others who were there at the time too.

So, without further ado, and with no timeline whatsoever and in no particular order....

A world-famous Scottish piano soloist was playing with one of the orchestras in Glasgow, and after he'd finished his concerto to tumultuous applause from a packed auditorium, he began playing his encore - a solo piece, the middle of which included a short "jazzy" section.

As this jazzy bit of the encore started, one of the extra players in the double bass section, who was a total, die-hard jazz fan himself, suddenly perked up, picked up his instrument and started playing along, much to the astonishment of everyone on the stage, the soloist included.

The pianist's music was all written down and wasn't improvised in any way, so when the bassist unexpectedly joined in, it completely put the soloist off his stride. He then seemed to get stuck in a sort of a loop which he couldn't get out of, as the bassist zoned out of reality and into Jazz World, *pizzicato*-ing a walking bass line to his heart's content, and more or less taking all the attention away from the front of the stage and drawing it straight to his dumbfounded section, as unwelcome as it was.

Starky would not have been happy at all with the breaking of his Rule Number One had he been there, and after that concert, I don't recall seeing the bassist in question again in that particular orchestra.

Oops.

Normally, it's great, but in this instance, Jazz sucks.

Which is, no doubt, what the now-rubbed bassist also thinks.

***

At a concert in Edinburgh's Usher Hall in the mid to late nineties, I was in the section for "Belshazzar's Feast", William Walton's epic cantata which features a large orchestra and an even larger chorus.

The leader of the orchestra for that concert was a pal whom I'd known for decades, both through work and socialising, and also through playing football together for various orchestral teams over the years.

At the break in the afternoon rehearsal before the evening concert, both the orchestra and the chorus left the stage at the same time, desperate for a coffee or something stronger, and there was a great mass of bodies clogging up the two small doors either side of the Usher Hall's concert platform.

My pal found himself right behind me, at the back of the crowd trying to get off the stage and started – for a joke – pushing me from behind (still holding his violin) and swearing at me, calling me all the names under the sun, as though that would make the throng speed up their exit.

"Come on, you! Get a f*****g move on, you f*****g c**t! Move your fat ar*e, you tw*t! It's always f*****g you, holding everyone up as usual you f*****g b*ll-end! AND I could hear you during the rehearsal. You were sh*te! What the f**k were you doing? I've heard some p*sh in my time but your performance there takes the f*****g biscuit! A*******e!"

Sometimes we have a bit of light-hearted banter like this with each other, but this time it was different.

Not because it was overly offensive, which it wasn't, believe it or not, but it was different this time because I was in fact, still in the percussion section at the back of the stage, having a look at some notes, and totally oblivious to some innocent singer from the chorus who looked like me from behind, apparently, being pushed around, verbally lambasted and sworn at by the leader of the orchestra.

The singer turned around.

"I presume you're speaking to me?" he said indignantly.

The leader's jaw dropped and he profusely apologised. "I'm so sorry, I thought you were someone else...."

And as if that wasn't bad enough, he later gave me a hard time because it wasn't me!

We're still good pals and anyway, it's always very funny in my world, the old case of mistaken identity faux-pas.

The great kn*****d.

***

I, and most of my colleagues could fill a whole chapter with the bizarre drivel we've heard coming from conductors, both in rehearsals and outside of them over the last thirty years. I've already touched on some Ballet classics from the podium, and things like one particular "maestro" asking the first violins "At this point, could I have more of a sense of wonderment, please?" doesn't really help their cause.

As a percussionist/timpanist, the sentence we hear the most from conductors (apart from the ones who are or were percussionists themselves, and therefore know better) is "Could you use harder sticks?"

One supposedly top-class conductor used this favourite phrase of theirs one time, as I struggled with a tuning issue when one of my drums decided to play up and started slipping a bit, basically de-tuning itself as I was playing it and consequently winding me up no end.

At the break, the conductor came over to me, wanting to know what the problem was. I explained that the instrument was playing up and assured him that I would have it sorted and everything would be fine by the evening's concert.

He thought for a second and said "Tell you what, Martin. We'll do that same passage when we restart after the break, but this time, use harder sticks."

If you're not aware of how this works, I can easily explain it by saying that the tuning of an instrument is not affected in any way whatsoever by whatever it's played with. You can hit a timp with a soft stick, a hard stick or a recently-deceased halibut. You'll get the same note every time. It's the same as saying to a pianist "The Middle C on the piano is out of tune – could you use your fourth finger on it, instead of your third?"

Anyway, I felt there was no point in explaining this to the great maestro, and so, when we restarted the rehearsal, he looked over and I reached around to my stick case behind me, found my hard sticks, held them up on display for him, and as we started playing, he nodded over with a thumbs-up and a look of self-satisfaction that he had fixed the problem.

What I didn't tell him, though, was that I'd pulled the age-old drummer's trick, used since time began to satisfy the whims of the mighty and the easily-fooled.

When I reached around for my sticks, I deliberately picked up the exact same pair I'd been using before the break, and with confidence, showed them as though they were the new ones chosen by the mighty maestro.

Drummers - 1, Idiots - 0

***

China and Taiwan, 2000

I've always summed up the BBC SSO's first China tour in one word – interesting. To this day, I still don't know if I actually enjoyed it, but it was certainly an experience I'm glad I had, and it was most definitely interesting.

I don't mean it in the way of the ancient Chinese curse, "May you live in interesting times", just that it was genuinely interesting.

It was also interesting for one of the Chinese organisers of the tour, but possibly in a much more serious way, although I'll probably never know.

After the last concert on mainland China before we jetted off to Taiwan the following day, the tour organisers held a reception for the orchestra, with all the usual drinks and canapés, which was much appreciated by everyone.

One of the tour organisers, a Chinese lady in her late thirties or early forties, wearing a smart business suit and carrying a programme from the evening's concert, approached me with a very courteous "Hello".

"Hello," I replied. "Thank you for this wonderful reception!"

"Ah, you're welcome, but I have a question, please..."

"Certainly, what is it?"

She opened the programme to a picture of an orchestra with "BBC SSO" printed underneath it.

The lady then pointed to the printed letters and asked "What is that 'S' for?"

I looked at the photo and thought something wasn't quite right with it.

On closer inspection, I realised that I recognised only a few of the people in it, and that it was in fact a photograph of the London-based BBC Symphony Orchestra, the "BBC SO".

"It stands for 'Scottish'," I said.

She looked at me silently and seemed confused.

I pointed around the room at everyone and said politely "BBC SCOTTISH Symphony Orchestra, yes? The photo is of the BBC Symphony Orchestra, not of this orchestra"

The lady's face went ashen, as all the colour drained out of it. She muttered a little, quiet "Oh...", turned and walked silently away.

Were they expecting the BBC SO? Was it just a small photographic mix-up? Did she get into major trouble?

As I said, I'll never know, but by the look on her face, it didn't appear to be a trivial matter, and I've always hoped she was ok and things didn't turn out too bad for her.

***

Dave Lyons, my partner in crime since music college days, and who's just admitted that he didn't know that "they made shoes in half sizes, like an eight-and-a-half" and always wondered why he's had sore feet for forty-eight years...said the funniest ever two-word phrase.

The two everyday words in question are innocuous and banal in their normal usage, but put into a certain situation, they took on the mantle of being the most hilariously unexpected two words I've ever heard.

It was at 1pm and lunchtime in London, just as a few of us left the Royal Albert Hall after our morning rehearsal for that evening's Prom concert in August 2016, that Dave said "I'm just going to get a Burger King for lunch and take it back to my hotel room, so I'll see you guys later."

We all had lunch together minus Dave, went our separate ways, killed time in the afternoon, met up again and had dinner, played the concert, went to a bar afterwards, went to the hotel bar when the previous bar closed and went to bed, only to get up again the next morning in time for another 10am to 1pm rehearsal back at the RAH.

At the rehearsal, Dave said "I was starving when I got back to my room after the hotel bar last night!"

"Did you order food from room service?" I asked.

"No, I had almost a full packet of Burger King fries left over from lunchtime," he replied.

"Dave, that's bloody disgusting!" I said with a grimace. "Cold Burger King chips?! Yuck!"

"Oh, they weren't cold," he said.

"How come they weren't cold?" I asked Dave, puzzled.

"Hair dryer."

"Oh, my god," I wheezed, when I eventually stopped laughing. "You heated them up with the hair dryer in your room?! How did they taste?"

"Bloody amazing!" said the Grand Gourmet of Haute Cuisine with a cheeky grin.

As unexpected answers go, I don't think that anyone could have predicted that one, but I have to award the prize for a person speechless for the longest time after an unexpected answer, to one particular musician who innocuously said to a much older colleague, as they passed in a corridor backstage, "Hi, Lucy, that's a nice jumper you're wearing."

"Thanks," came the reply. "I bought it with the money I saved from not having to buy tampons after my hysterectomy."

***

The best ever "claim to fame" goes to the ex-Principal Horn of the Scottish Ballet Orchestra, Terry Johns, known as "Drac" since his student days.

Drac's book, "Letters From Lines and Spaces" is a well-documented journey through his distinguished career and definitely well worth a read.

That's not his best claim to fame, though.

When Drac was Principal Horn of the LSO, he played on a lot of the soundtracks of blockbuster movies of the time, most notably "Superman" and "Star Wars", and as the scene unfolds of Anakin (who became Darth Vader) Skywalker's funeral pyre being lit by his son, Luke in "Star Wars: Episode VI - Return of the Jedi", it's Drac who's playing the solo horn part over the iconic images.

He told me that at a reception after an LSO concert in the mid-eighties, as he passed his friend John Wallace, the orchestra's legendary Principal Trumpet, he overheard one of the hosts of the reception ask "So, John, is it true that you were the solo trumpeter at Prince Charles and Lady Diana's wedding?"

"Yes, it is…" he replied.

Before he could continue though, Drac interjected as he passed.

"That's nothing," he said in his lilting Welsh accent. "I played at Darth Vader's funeral!"

***

The Funniest Sound I've Ever Heard

Something that I've never done is to keep a count of how many gigs I've played, but for this bit I've had to get last year's diary out and count them up, as sad as it is.

So, in 2017, from 1st January to 31st December, I had one hundred and thirty-three concerts or performances. Most of these had from one to six days of rehearsals beforehand, and I was also involved in over thirty recording sessions (I gave up counting at 31 sessions by October) for either CD or radio. Mainly orchestral sessions with all of the orchestras, but I've also included rock band stuff too.

In total, according to my diary, I had three hundred and eighty-seven sessions last year.

So, taking that as an average, that means that over the past thirty years of my professional life, I've had around eleven thousand, six hundred and ten sessions, approximately.

This total doesn't include the hundreds of hours teaching, going to concerts as a paying punter or anything else like that.

Taking the 11,610 sessions as the usual three-hour session length, although that obviously does vary, it gives an approximate total of thirty-four thousand, eight hundred and thirty hours of time spent listening to myself and other people make noise.

Out of all those 34,830 hours, the one sound that I will always remember is a sound that lasted for about a second.

It was a sound so special that I said to the person who made it "If I ever write a book, I'm including that".

Scottish Ballet's 2014/15 winter tour of Nutcracker had been plodding along nicely, with no major incidents or even anything worthy of a short footnote.

That was, until we reached Inverness, the ninth week of the eleven-week tour.

The orchestra pit of Eden Court theatre presents quite a few challenges to the band. We're spread around the pit strangely, with some sections squeezed together and other parts of the pit having large areas of unused space. The percussion and timp sections are at the back as usual, but in this instance, around three feet lower than the rest of the orchestra. Our biggest challenge here is trying to see the conductor through the legs of the trombone section and around a few of the many steel girders that gives the pit the appearance of - and us the impression of playing in - a submarine.

To illustrate how much headroom the pit offers, the brass and woodwind can't physically stand up for the bows at the end of the show due to the proximity of the low pit ceiling.

I've always maintained that in the Eden Court pit, everyone sitting in front of the trombones would benefit from wearing ear plugs, and everyone sitting behind the trombones, i.e. us, could do with some nose plugs, as our faces are perfectly level with their toxic waste outlets, as it were.

To the right of the trombones sit the woodwind section, and that section's player furthest away from me is the bass clarinetist, Alan Bacchetti. He had been suffering from a bit of a cold for the past week and was sitting around twelve feet away from me across one of the pit's empty spaces.

Mid-way through the second act, there is the 'Divertissement: le Chocolat', also known as the Spanish Dance.

After a four-bar introduction in a quick tempo, the trumpet plays the melody for sixteen bars, after which the majority of the orchestra join in and repeat it at a much stronger dynamic.

With a septuplet upbeat into the fourteenth bar of the trumpet tune, Alan joins in, with a *crescendo* to *double forte* on a held note and as the bass clarinet is a fairly large wind instrument, it requires a large lung-full of air to achieve all of this.

Alan, another of the funniest people I know, a brilliant story-teller and always great company - and a very fine player - had his instrument at the ready, counting the bars before his entry.

Ten,

Eleven,

Twelve,
(Massive breath),
Then it happened.

At the absolute exact moment of the first note of the fast seven in the upbeat, the viruses of Alan's winter cold decided to go rogue. They all went haywire, and he accidentally coughed a full pair of lung's-worth of air - every last molecule - into his bass clarinet, all in one upbeat, as his fingers automatically played the septuplet.

The resulting sound almost stopped the show - literally - as the rest of the orchestra, especially the wind, actually did stop playing for a fraction of a second, the shock manifesting itself in brief bewilderment and confusion, feelings which were immediately replaced by almost uncontrollable hysterics.

Players were actually crying while playing, myself included.

The sound itself is, of course impossible to recreate, as even the low pit ceiling helped to amplify its weird, primitive, ear-splitting howling scream straight to the back of the auditorium.

The closest thing I could compare it to would have to be an incident from the late Cretaceous period, as a fully-grown Tyrannosaurus Rex emerges from the treeline of a dense forest and into a deserted, peaceful prehistoric glade, whereupon it lumbers to the edge of a large pool of cool, clear water, surveys the clearing and seeing no threats, bends over to take a drink.

The sound that Alan made that evening wasn't the same beautifully rounded tone that he'd been making flawlessly every night for the past eight weeks, evoking visions of sun, sangria and flamenco dancing. It was in fact, identical to the sound the unsuspecting T. Rex makes as it is violently and painfully rectally impaled on the horns of a previously hidden, enraged, charging Triceratops.

***

I won the best ever first prize at a karaoke once, but I don't remember singing in it.

It was once again in Inverness, on tour with SB.

After an evening performance on a two-show Thursday, most of the orchestra went to our regular haunt in Inverness, and after a while and a lot of alcohol, we headed to a bar called 'Barbazzar', situated almost on the banks of the River Ness. Someone had discovered that it was hosting a rock karaoke that evening, and as there were quite a few of us who often participated in these things when we were on tour, we all went along, all of us at various levels of sobriety.

I was really quite drunk.

Not something of which I'm proud, but for the sake of complete honesty, I have to admit it.

We arrived at Barbazzar and immediately ordered more drink, as if we'd not had enough already. A few of us put our names down for the karaoke and after a while, my name was called to go up and sing the Stereophonics' hit "Local Boy in the Photograph."

I struggled through it, offending any Stereophonics fans in the bar with my out of tune, embarrassing effort and after it was over, I headed back to the bar for more drink. As I stood there, happily increasing my chances of severe alcohol poisoning with gay abandon, I listened to my friend and colleague, 'cellist Rosie Townhill, sing an immaculate rendition of Prince's "Kiss."

Rosie is a lovely, petite and ever-optimistic girl - and a massive fan of Doctor Who - who admits to often having "blonde moments", which makes her all the more likeable and funny.

In the past, we've done the odd duet at karaoke, but we haven't for some time now, as our last performance in Jonny Fox's bar (in Inverness again) didn't go particularly well due to our musical differences.

The song was "Especially For You" by Kylie Minogue and Jason Donovan, and our differences were that Rosie was sober and knew all the words, and I wasn't and didn't know any of the words.

Anyway, as Rosie finished the Prince number to massive applause from the busy bar, I finished my drink and went upstairs to the gents.

As I stood there, swaying gently, the door opened and a guy came in and stood at the urinal three away from mine. He was in his late-twenties, around five feet six or seven, wearing a white, sleeveless t-shirt which showed off his amateur-looking tattoos on his wiry but well-defined lower arms.

I don't normally make a habit of checking out the physique of the bloke next to me in the toilet, but I took it all in in a split second when he suddenly yelled with obvious pent-up aggression and punched the wall hard with his free hand.

He turned to me and said "Do I look angry?" in a menacing growl.

I thought *I'm not joining in with this,* and I said, "Yeah, you do, but I'm not interested, mate. I'm here for a good night out and a laugh, and I'm not interested, so if you're after a bit of trouble you'll need to look somewhere else."

I remember saying that, because I had instantly sobered up with a feeling of imminent dread that it was all about to kick off.

"No, no," he said, shaking his head, "It's not you. It's a guy downstairs, one of my group. He's insulted a female friend and I'm going to kill him!"

"Nah, you don't want to do that, mate" I said, relieved. "You know that'll only get you into more trouble."

To cut a long story short, I spent the next fifteen minutes or so, talking him out of killing his pal - now ex-pal - downstairs.

The guy seemed pretty unhinged and said he was a cage fighter, which I was dubious about, but he assured me that he had a televised fight against "a guy from Dunfermline" coming up in a few weeks' time. It must have been obvious that I thought he was fantasising, so he told me in gory detail what he was going to do to him when the fight arrived which, to be honest, I really didn't want to hear.

I listened to him rant on anyway, out of a sense of politeness and also a nagging suspicion that if I didn't, there was a good chance that he'd start practicing his rather unpleasant-sounding moves on me right there.

He eventually calmed down and I thankfully didn't hear any commotion or witness any fracas when we went back downstairs and re-joined our respective groups, so all was good.

Alan Friel, our Second Trumpet came over.

"Where have you been?" he said, excitedly. "They've been calling out your name!"

"I've been upstairs preventing a blood-bath", I said and started to fill him in on my last fifteen minutes of drunken peace-brokering.

Alan stopped me after about three seconds and said "You've won!"

"I've won what?"

"The karaoke! The guy's been calling you for ages… go and see him!"

"Karaoke?" I was confused. "But I don't remem…." I looked at the guy in charge of the karaoke just as he saw me and called me over the microphone.

"Martin! Come and get your prize!" he said with a big smile.

I walked over to his area and all I remember about it is him saying "I've never seen anyone look like a Ribena berry trying to reach the high notes before!" and laughing.

So, the reason that I won wasn't due to my amazing vocal dexterity, but because my face went blackcurrant-esque in the upper register.

Thanks, dude.

Back at the hotel the next morning, in the twin room I'd been given to myself, I awoke with a groan at the daylight coming in through the open curtains which I'd forgotten to close before going to bed the previous night.

As I looked at my travel bag sitting on the other bed, I noticed a couple of things that caught my attention and which really confused me.

The first was a double CD which I'd never seen before - "Anthology" by The Ramones.

What the….? I was totally puzzled by this. I'd never bought a Ramones CD in my life. *What's this doing here?*

Then I noticed a white envelope marked "Winner", next to my bag on the bed and I started to remember the previous evening's events. They were coming in little flashes, but I then remembered the karaoke guy saying "Here's your prize. It's from the sponsors of tonight's karaoke!" and handing me the CD and the envelope.

The latter was still unopened, so I slowly fumbled with it, clumsily trying to open it like an arthritic prestidigitator.

Eventually I got it open and pulled out its contents, a postcard-sized bit of paper with "£25" written on it

"Wow!" I said out loud.

I then said "WOW!" again, much louder when I saw who the sponsors of the karaoke were.

I had won a £25 gift voucher for Inverness' newly opened, first ever Fetish Shop.

If you really must know, yes of course I went in.

I bought myself a 'classy' t-shirt with a bio-mechanical half human/half-robot on it, but I spent the rest on a small, black vinyl shoulder bag - very Punk - for Rosie, because I did remember her brilliant singing and I genuinely thought that she should have won.

And anyway, out of all the items in the shop, it was also the least inappropriate thing I could have bought her.

**

It's been well documented many times in movies and literature over the years, that during the American involvement in the Vietnam War during the sixties and seventies, the veteran troops already serving there mostly did not make any effort to learn the names of the new recruits being constantly sent to reinforce them. This wasn't out of any maliciousness but used by the troops as a self-preservation mechanism. "Why bother learning his name? The less I know about him, the easier it'll be to handle when he goes and gets himself killed and replaced with another new guy."

Some musicians, with great irony, have compared this attitude to orchestral musicians' relationships with guest conductors.

"Who's conducting your orchestra this week?"

"No idea - some new guy, and it'll be someone different again next week. It's like bloody Vietnam."

Personally, I think that given a choice between spending a few years in the jungles of South-East Asia in the early seventies, with its long list of different ways to gruesomely die and a massive, ever-increasing body-count, or working for a week with a slightly inferior conductor who's a bit annoying, the Vietnam option possibly seems to be the tad less attractive one.

I can, however appreciate the dark humour in this misguided comparison, and I too can admit to many weeks of working without ever knowing the conductor's name.

He or she is the one person we, as players, must constantly watch - unfortunately, sometimes - and is simultaneously the only person on stage who's not making a sound, and the one person on stage most capable of destroying a performance single-handedly.

My best friend, Anne, is a 'cellist with the BBC SSO.

During the break in the first rehearsal of a new week and a new programme of repertoire, she was standing backstage and chatting with a new colleague in the orchestra, a young musician whom she'd never seen before, this being his first time working with that orchestra.

"Hi, you're a 'cellist, aren't you?" he asked pleasantly.

"Hello," replied Anne with a lovely smile. "Yes, I am. What do you do?" she asked.

"I'm the conductor," he said, deflated.

"Oh...."

Anne had just been playing for a full ninety minutes, with the young conductor standing eight feet away, right in front of her, waving his arms about and even talking directly to the 'cello section on more than two occasions.

Now, that is indeed impressive, and worthy of a Medal of Honor and a massed salute from the United States Marine Corps.

Even if the players do know the conductor's name, there are a lot of them who are referred to only by their nicknames.

Players can reply with any of the following when asked "So, who's conducting this week?"

It could be the Russian maestro, all-round nice guy and Frankie Howerd lookalike, Vassily Sinaisky, better known by a genius word-play on his name – Vaseline-me Nicely.

Or it could be any one of these examples with whom I've worked and are, for better or for worse: The Swiss Clock, Bob Hope, Olivier Newton-John, The Great Charlatan, Tricky Dicky, The Smiling Assassin, The Hooded Crow, Father Ted, Lah-de-dah Gunner Graham, and Aardvark.

I can take credit for only one of these names, and I'm not telling you which one.

Alright, it's Bob Hope.

My favourite though, is the name given to a guest conductor who appeared briefly with Scottish Ballet.

Diminutive in stature but colossal in ego, he exuded a behaviour on the podium which was, frankly, hugely disrespectful towards the orchestra in favour of his own distorted self-image, and a conducting technique that caused him to resemble a minute version of one of those giant, inflatable men that you see blowing about outside car showrooms.

Anyway, he's now and always will be known by the name he's been christened by our woodwind section.

Flappotron.

***

For the opening sequence of Stanley Kubrik's horror movie, "The Shining", the great director used the "Dies Irae" section of "Dream of a Witches' Sabbath", the last movement from Berlioz's "Symphony Fantastique".

This section opens ominously with two solo bass bells, a C and - a fourth lower - a G, signalling the start of the Dies Irae as the epic piece nears its conclusion.

To be technical for a moment and revert to percussionist jargon, the offstage bell part goes "two 'Dings' on the C and one 'Dong' on the low G".

So, that's:

DING....

DING....

DONG....

Easy.

These massive, eight or nine feet tall tubular bells are played offstage, with the percussionist – including myself at six feet two inches – having to use a ladder to be able to reach them.

The bonus of playing that part is that the offstage player is usually able to get changed out of his or her concert gear before the piece finishes and get to the pub before everyone else.

The drawback of playing this offstage part though, is that it's notorious for things going wrong with it.

The player has to be in total control of the bells and absolutely in tempo, or it sounds dreadful and can easily result in an undeserved roasting from the conductor.

Being so far away from the rest of the orchestra and through a set of doors is a challenge in itself, but the biggest issue we have with this part is, because of the proximity of our ears to the actual bells, and because we're playing them really loudly, we can't physically hear anything else as soon as we start playing, and it can easily become very wrong very quickly.

Sometimes we have our own offstage conductor who will be watching the onstage one and trying his best to synchronize with his tempo. At other times we might be on our own with a television monitor, but that can sometimes be worse if the screen has a half-second delay or suchlike.

The SNO played this piece in the late '80s with a conductor who, for no reason, took a dislike to the player on this part, and gave him a hard time for the whole week of rehearsals prior to the first concert.

"Offstage bells! What are you doing?!" was an oft-repeated phrase that week.

The player in question was Starky, and his Rule Number One - "Don't draw attention to yourself" - was about to be taken to a whole new level.

To be fair to my friend, he was an innocent victim of a conductor's ego-trip and had done nothing wrong at all to warrant this continuous tirade.

Even so, nothing Starky did that week was good enough for this particular conductor, one of the rudest men on the circuit, and so both of them were not in the best of moods as they arrived at Dundee's Caird Hall for the first concert of the week.

The hall is a massive building, which the orchestra used for all their CD recordings at that time due to its excellent acoustics, a product of its classic 'shoe-box' shape.

Even at the afternoon's rehearsal, Starky got a hard time over something that the conductor invented, and to put it mildly, I reckon Starky probably removed him from his Christmas card list after that week.

At the dinner break before the concert, he was fuming.

"I can't wait to get this week finished and see the back of that conductor!"

Although I'm paraphrasing, as I seem to remember that he didn't use the word "conductor".

Anyway, the second half arrived, as Starky walked offstage to his bells and the great maestro walked on and started Symphony Fantastique.

All was going well as the fifth and final movement began, and as the Witches' Dance approached, Starky climbed up his ladder and watched his own personal offstage conductor like a hawk.

The bell solo arrived and the offstage conductor cued Starky – *Go!*

With great aplomb, Starky, to use another percussion technical term, knocked the shit out of it.

And of all the moments in time,

DING....

it was at this precise moment

DING....

that the string holding the bottom G bell

DO..

broke.

The huge metal instrument dropped from its frame and, like a giant pogo-stick with an invisible rider, bounced down a flight of concrete stairs.

Each ear-splitting "*DONG*" actually got louder with every impact, the Caird Hall's amazing acoustics amplifying them into the auditorium, before the bell eventually slowly toppled over, like a felled metal tree and onto the marble floor, with a sound reminiscent of a delivery of scaffolding from the back of a tipper truck.

The conductor's face was scarlet with rage.

The rest of the orchestra's faces were contorted in badly-suppressed hysterical laughter.

Starky, still up the ladder and who could only watch powerlessly, as half of his compliment of bass bells bounced away down the stairs, did what every other professional would do.

He shrugged his shoulders and carried on.

After all, he still had a lot more entries to play, although they now went

DING....

DING....

....

Chapter Seventeen

Coda

My Graduation Day was in July 1987, and although I did a Post-graduate year after that, I spent more of it working professionally than I did studying at the RSAMD, so I've always counted July '87 as my official entry into professional life.

Margaret Thatcher was the Prime Minister, and the British Army were still on the streets and in the fields of Northern Ireland.

Belfast was still a regular stop on Scottish Ballet's circuit, although back then, the company put all of us - orchestra, dancers, tech crew, management - up in the same hotel, as they felt it wasn't too safe for us to be booking our own accommodation in Belfast at that time.

The 'safe' hotel they booked us into for years was the Europa, right opposite the Grand Opera House where we were playing.

It was the most-bombed hotel in the world.

It had just recently knocked the Beirut Hilton off the Number One slot for the dubious honour.

Next to the theatre was the offices of the Ulster Unionist party, and the IRA (allegedly) would often leave car bombs outside it, blowing it up, and as collateral damage, also blowing in the windows of the theatre, the Europa and The Crown Bar too.

On several tours, we were the first company back in the theatre after one of these explosions, and one time in particular, we had to use portacabins as changing rooms while the usual ones were being repaired after a particularly large blast.

A tactic of the paramilitaries at the time was to report multiple car bombs around the city to the authorities, and while the police and army were distracted checking them out, they could then move people, weapons or whatever more safely for a few hours.

I was sharing a twin room with Big Ian during one of these city lockdowns, with six suspected car bombs having been simultaneously reported all over Belfast.

Around 4pm one sunny Friday in February 1991 - my first Swan Lake tour - I remember both of us hanging out the window of our tenth-floor room in the Europa, watching a cordoned-off white transit van parked on the empty street below us.

After a while, an army robot appeared from around a corner, controlled by a hidden soldier, watching via its front-mounted camera. Slowly moving on its caterpillar tracks, it manoeuvred into position at the van's back doors.

A few seconds later there was a small "bang!" as the robot blew the locks off the doors. It very slowly opened one door, reached in with its arm and pulled out a large brown sack, dropping it on the ground in front of the doors before retreating around the corner and out of sight once more.

Around ten minutes later, a soldier appeared from around the same corner.

He slowly walked up to the sack lying on the ground and looked at it intently for a good ten seconds.

Then, to our complete disbelief, he kicked it.

Nothing happened.

I'm sure he knew what he was doing, but I'll always remember both that and the shocked look on Ian's face, mirroring my own, as he did it.

At other times, I'd be walking down the street and spot the barrel of a rifle sticking out from behind the corner of a building, an obvious sign of an army patrol. I must admit, I always used to cough loudly as I approached those corners, announcing my presence as a safeguard against accidentally surprising the gun's possibly twitchy owner.

Things have obviously changed a lot in thirty years, the political transformation of Northern Ireland being an obvious testament to that.

On a very much less dramatic level, the world of orchestral playing has also massively transformed, although as the well-used expression goes, some things never change.

I can only speak for my own observations here, and it's probable that not everyone would agree with them. If you ask a sixty-piece orchestra their view on a conductor, it's highly likely that you would get sixty different opinions.

For me, the biggest change I've noticed is the standard of playing. It just keeps getting better all the time.

Pam, the ex-Principal Percussion with the RSNO and my former teacher at the RSAMD, recently asked me to adjudicate at a percussion competition at the Junior department of the now RCS.

The candidates were all still school pupils, their ages ranging from thirteen to eighteen years old.

One of them - a fifteen-year old - played a piece that I played for my final recital after three years at senior Academy when I was twenty-one!

The advent of the digital age has played a great part in this explosion of standard, especially YouTube.

There you can find hundreds of lessons and tutorials on any instrument you can think of, videos of inspirational performances, close-up/slow-motion technique guides and a million other things to be used by any student, young or old, and a plethora of websites and online forums are also available to answer any question from keen, curious minds.

Players in orchestras come and go, and the personnel and orchestra list at the back of concert programmes is always changing as they retire, pass away, leave to join other bands, leave the profession to do something else entirely different or leave for a myriad of other reasons, sometimes not of their own choosing.

Sometimes they leave because they've been overtaken by the rising standard. It doesn't happen a lot, but it does happen often enough to keep the rest of us on our guard.

The overwhelmingly vast majority of players are very amiable and great to be around, but as in any profession, not everyone is nice to work with.

Massive egos are still on display in most of the orchestras, and although the players exhibiting them are very much in the minority, they're still there, and even though they are all uniformly despised by the majority, I don't see that side of things changing any time soon, unfortunately. That will always be human nature, I think and we just have to put up with and adapt to it.

The Scottish Ballet Orchestra is an extremely pleasant exception to the egomania, I've always found, as outwith our tours we're all freelance players, which I think is a great leveller amongst us.

I have to admit that I haven't worked with Scottish Opera for some time now, as their tours tend to coincide with SB's, but I have many times in the past, and I do know a lot of really lovely people from the OSO, so I'm sure that they too are still ego-free.

The well-documented two most common complaints from players are money and hours, and contrary to some beliefs from outside of the profession, you will never become financially rich by playing in an orchestra.

In 2017, the average yearly salary of a rank and file violinist at the BBC SSO was around the £30,000 mark before tax. Not a lot when compared to other professions.

It's also not a lot when it includes the all anti-social hours that musicians work. We're other people's entertainment, so we don't have weekends for a start.

Or the hours spent practicing on a free day for the following week's programme.

Or the hours spent travelling to and from concerts.

Or the days and nights spent worrying that you're not good enough, full of self-doubt and hyper self-criticism, either about something you've just played or something that you're about to play.

A fellow freelancer told me of a concert he did with an orchestra at the London Proms a few years ago. The orchestra in question had a sponsorship deal with a train company, so that meant they didn't have to pay travel allowance to the players. The hotel was provided, with no opt-out clause, so that meant they didn't have to pay accommodation to the players either. Because their rehearsal was at 10am on the day of the evening concert, out of necessity everyone travelled down the day before and travelled back home the day after the concert.

So, after leaving at 10.30am on Monday morning and arriving back home at 5pm on Wednesday evening, the player received £95 - a normal concert fee at the time.

Try getting a plumber or any other tradesman to come out to your house for three days for that amount.

Every orchestra is different too, and each has their own style of playing. Trumpeter Robert Baxter, another of the busiest freelancers in the country said something to me that sums up a lot.

"As freelancers we have to be adaptable. If you're not adaptable, you're not employable."

This has always been the case, and as the personnel in each orchestra changes, the organic creature that is the orchestra itself changes with it and these days as standards constantly improve, we have to be more adaptable than ever while still trying to stay on top of our game.

An example of this adaptability that many freelance players use, concerns some differences between the two symphony orchestras in Scotland, the BBC SSO and the RSNO. At climaxes in the music or at the end of pieces which have pauses requiring everyone to watch the conductor and play the final chord or chords together as one, the BBC SSO play almost directly (but not quite) with the conductor's downbeat, whereas the RSNO have quite a marked delay before they play. Neither way is the right way or the wrong way, they're just different in their approach but it takes quite a bit of getting used to if you've only been used to playing one way or the other, and if you're not immediately adaptable at speed and quick to learn and implement the change, there's a good chance you won't be back in again.

All of the Scottish orchestras are now housed in different homes from thirty years ago.

The RSNO have a new, purpose-built home adjoining the GRCH where they rehearse, record and give concerts.

The BBC SSO has moved from the old BBC Scotland building on Queen Margaret Drive to its new home in a greatly renovated City Halls. Sadly, the BBC Club has also gone, disappearing into the ether when the new BBC Scotland building opened at Pacific Quay on the banks of the River Clyde.

The Orchestra of Scottish Opera have had a few different rehearsal venues over the years, now rehearsing mainly in Hillington, and the Scottish Ballet Orchestra usually now rehearse at SB's new headquarters adjoining the Tramway on Glasgow's south side, although we also often vary our rehearsal venue.

As I write this, the SCO, based in Edinburgh are building a new concert hall and home for themselves as they too prepare to move, out of the old Queen's Hall.

But don't take just my word for all of this!

I asked some colleagues if they would like to contribute to this chapter, and to say what has changed for them over the past thirty or so years, along with any personal highlights in that time.

And because they are all extremely nice, kind and lovely people, and absolutely outstanding musicians, they all immediately agreed.

They have all spanned the same years as me, or close enough and are all musicians whom I genuinely admire and greatly respect.

Here are their thoughts, each written in their own individual styles and unaltered by me.

I must say at this point, and you'll have to trust me on this, but I deliberately wrote the preceding words of this chapter before reading any of the following contributions, and I've found what they've said to be very interesting indeed.

John Gracie - Principal Trumpet, Royal Scottish National Orchestra for 35 years (retired 2016), now successfully freelancing

Positive changes:

The standard of orchestral playing has risen considerably over the last three or four decades which it has had to do to keep up with the modern repertoire which is now thrown at us.

"Free day" schemes have been introduced but the time off varies a lot between orchestras and indeed within individual orchestras themselves.

Rehearsal venues and indeed concert halls have improved considerably. Some have been purpose built and others adapted to suit much bigger orchestras, although changing facilities in some are still pretty poor, i.e. Glasgow, Edinburgh and Perth.

There are now many more overseas tours on the work schedules, which is good for the orchestras but not always good for members with families to look after. Some, but not all managers are sympathetic in allowing time off for family reasons.

Negative changes:

Salaries/freelance fees have not kept up with other professions. Travel allowances to out of town venues have not kept up with train prices. Petrol and parking costs are well above the allowances negotiated by the Musicians Union.

Most extra fees for radio, tv and commercial recordings have now been incorporated into the basic session fees which have been eroded over the years.

Accommodation costs are now much higher than the allowances given by orchestras, forcing musicians to book an inferior standard of hotels.

It takes far too long nowadays for Orchestra vacancies to be filled. Too many people are on the audition panels and decisions take too long to be made.

Highlights

Some of the personal highlights in the last 30 years in the RSNO have been European Tours with WALTER WELLER. Dozens of recordings with NEEME JARVI (Strauss, Mahler, Shostakovich, etc.)

***

Martyn Brabbins - Associate Principal Conductor of the BBC Scottish Symphony Orchestra 1994-2005, currently Music Director, English National Opera.

It has been my huge privilege to have spent more of my time conducting in Scotland than in any other part of the world. I first raised a baton before the BBC SSO in October 1991, in the orchestra's former long-term home on Queen Margaret Drive, opposite the beautiful Botanic Gardens, and close to the wonderful charm of Glasgow's West End.

One of the myriad changes in Scottish musical life since 1991 is of course the move made by the SSO to its new permanent home in Glasgow's splendidly refurbished City Halls. This move, masterminded by Hugh MacDonald, then Director of the orchestra, with support from the City of Glasgow and the BBC, has transformed the life and activities of the SSO, and made a big impact on the lives of the musicians in the orchestra. The Scottish Chamber Orchestra also benefit from the splendid atmosphere of the City Halls with their regular series of Glasgow concerts.

Every orchestra is on a constant journey of evolution, and the SSO has certainly seen a huge turnover of personnel in the period I have been working with them. But, the identity of the orchestra remains as strong and individual as it always has.

The SSO in so many ways has gone from strength to strength. The recording profile of the orchestra is now well established, particularly through the relationship with the Hyperion label. This relationship was in an embryonic stage back in the early 1990s and now is a regular feature in the working life of the SSO.

Similarly, I know the RSNO have a very healthy recording life, in part due to the legacy of Neemi Järvi, who made many wonderful recordings with that orchestra.

Touring is a very special part of any orchestra's life, and I have been fortunate enough to have travelled abroad quite regularly with various orchestras, including the SSO. The orchestra has a healthy international profile - linked partly to the successes of their recordings, to the relationships with their eminent Chief Conductors, and to touring organisations and concert venues who all recognise the quality and excitement to be had from a BBC SSO concert.

Again, Scotland's other orchestras also have strong international reputations, and for a country with a relatively small population, it's probably fair to say that Scotland does punch above its musical weight.

The fact that the SSO is a public service broadcasting orchestra, supported incredibly generously by the BBC, it allows the orchestra to programme in a very bold and adventurous manner.

Ilan Volkov's "Tectonics" for instance, is truly ground-breaking. Rare performances of neglected operas by Birtwistle and Maxwell Davies could only be mounted by a BBC orchestra, and the SSO boldly go where no others have!

The City Halls then, as I mentioned earlier, has had a transformative effect on the SSO. Likewise, the RSNO's new rehearsal and recording facility adjacent to the Royal Concert Hall, has had a similarly positive impact on the day to day life of that orchestra. Not to be outdone, the SCO over in Edinburgh is in the process of building a brand new, state of the art concert hall. Something is clearly going well in the musical life of Scotland!

Having said that, one can but despair at the loss of the Chorus of Scottish Opera, and the reduction of the contract of the Orchestra of Scottish Opera.

As I am discovering in my own role as Music Director of ENO, opera is a challenging environment to work in, and the level of investment and funding involved in the production of world class opera performances is enormously high. Nonetheless, the loss of full time musical forces at Scottish Opera is something to be lamented.

Happily, the company is still creating excellent productions, widely admired and supported by Scottish audiences.

One other significant change in recent years has been the renaming of the RSAMD, now known as the Royal Conservatoire of Scotland. This change reflects the increased international reach of the institution, and the new level of ambition for music education in Scotland. An ambition that has seen the ground-breaking introduction of the "Sistema" system of instrumental tuition, based on the Venezuelan model. And it is at this grass-roots level where changes can have the most profound impact.

So, on reflection, there is so much to celebrate in Scottish musical life - and of course, I haven't even mentioned NYOS, NYCOS, or St Magnus, Lammermuir or Edinburgh Festivals, amateur music-making, fabulous brass bands, Hebrides and Red Note Ensembles!

One source of personal satisfaction for me is the success and relative longevity of the OCC (Orkney Conductor's Course) which I started in conjunction with Glenys Hughes at the St Magnus Festival some 15 years ago. This intensive conducting course has given opportunities and experience to 120-plus young conductors from all over the world and is recognised as one of the premier short conducting courses in Europe.

Having played a small part in this rich tapestry of music-making is a source of great pride and satisfaction for me, and I thank all the Scottish musicians, organisers and audiences who have made me welcome!

***

Robert Baxter - Independent Freelance Trumpet, 1989-present and recent Award-Winning Conductor.

When my good friend and colleague Martin asked me to contribute to his writings I was flattered and pleased. I did however feel less than pleased when he told me it was to mark 30 years working as freelance musicians although things did feel a little better when I realised that I had only been working for a mere 28 years; sorry Martin!

Whatever people may say about the music business, it is one place where you never get bored doing what we do. To spend time in the company of creative, artistic people, introverts and extroverts and sometimes a mixture of both, is guaranteed to make the schedule of rehearsals and concerts or recordings much more interesting.

Coupled with the fact that we are there playing instruments that we grew up with as children and now still get to do this as adults with some of the greatest and - occasionally - not the greatest music in the world, will never allow boredom or routine to set in. The variety of a full freelance schedule makes you flexible and adaptable and that variety can keep you fresh.

In recent years I find myself witnessing a large number of my elder colleagues retiring. These were the faces who welcomed me into the business, booked me for work and encouraged me and ultimately who I learnt from. As Brian Forshaw, one of a number of people who I enjoyed working with most and who was always so encouraging to me said, when he left the RSNO after, I think 35 years, it all goes so fast! Well, I'm beginning to see what he means now.

Martin asked me to write and to consider how things have changed in the music business. Up to this point they haven't changed much and perhaps they won't in the future either, as musicians will always have a desire to play music and hope audiences want come to listen. Perhaps how things have changed the most though is the speed of how we are booked and contacted by the various orchestras and managers. I used to quite enjoy getting home after a day's work to my flat in Mingarry street just off Queen Margaret Drive and walk round the curved hallway to see if the digital display on my answer machine was showing a number of recorded voice messages. This for many freelance players was the link to employment and a faulty answer machine was sometimes the cause of concern, as were flat-mates who scrubbed messages!

I've been lucky enough to teach on and off throughout my career and I'm frequently asked by senior students who are thinking of entering the profession what it is like and will they be good enough to succeed? I always tell them that it depends how they measure success and that while there are considerable high points, many musicians have possibly had low points too - rejection, disappointments and frustration can be a part of the journey. I would always suggest to students that a thick skin and an inner resolve are useful attributes. Above all, the courage to enter the profession is one I always admire.

It's difficult thinking back over many years about working in the business. There are of course highlights of concerts, venues and tours that are remembered and there are also great memories of playing alongside musicians whom I was taught by and whom I admired greatly. I've been fortunate enough to play many Prom concerts, Edinburgh Festival concerts, recordings, tv and radio broadcasts, and recall some great conductors and memorable performances among them. I remember equally fondly though, playing for the Council for Music in Hospitals and for Live Music Now as part of a youthful and enthusiastic brass quintet.

I suppose like any industry, competition can be fierce and you can only work and develop at your own pace. I've found myself saying to pupils of mine in an attempt to encourage and hopefully inspire that if you focus on trying to be a better musician tomorrow than you were today, then no one can ever criticise your best intentions.

Rachmaninov once said 'music is enough for a lifetime, but a lifetime is not enough for music.'

***

Jane Reid - Rank and File First Violin, Royal Scottish National Orchestra, 1978-present.

Having been a member of the RSNO for around 40 years, I feel very fortunate to be part of this orchestra and Scotland's musical community.

At the time I joined the SNO, as it was then, almost all of our work was classically based, with a regular pattern. A long winter season of concerts in Scotland's biggest cities, mostly of the Overture/Concerto/Symphony type, with Edinburgh Festival concerts, BBC proms, recordings and Musica Nova, our contemporary music festival. Tours were always a great adventure, my first experience of places abroad, burning the candle at both ends to fit in sightseeing and socialising amongst the travel, rehearsal and concert schedule.

Our own summer Proms season lasted around 5 or 6 weeks, concerts in Aberdeen, Dundee, Edinburgh and Glasgow, a veritable sight-reading marathon for a new young player. My eyes were out on stalks! In Glasgow, the Proms was a very special festival which I still miss. Held in the old Kelvin Hall Arena, the changing and tea bar facilities had the aroma of the elephants who were housed there during the Circus season.

The Scottish Opera orchestra had not yet been formed and the operas were divided up between the existing orchestras, which gave the SNO the chance to play for the largest scale operas. Der Rosencavalier, Pelléas et Mélisande and Wozzeck were amongst my favourites, it was a privilege to play them.

The orchestra was at its largest capacity but with a tiny staff, most of the budget seemed to go on getting the best possible soloists and conductors which brought the audiences in.

Moving to the present, our work now is much more diverse in repertoire and types of work. Concerts of film music, or indeed playing along with the movies on screen are amongst those that bring audiences in to experience live music that they know well. The RSNO is fortunate to have a fantastic new rehearsal facility attached to the Royal Concert Hall, a place where we can also stage lunchtime and chamber concerts.

Our education programme is more sophisticated, a CD for babies, nursery concerts, all ages of school children, plus working side by side with young instrumentalists, music students, adult musicians and composers.

We also play further afield in Scotland, travelling to outlying areas, often in smaller numbers to give people a chance to hear live music. Our staff has grown, a necessity with the increased diversity of our work and financial needs, Funding is a constant problem, from raising money for tours, to being able to fill vacant posts in orchestral ranks to affording the conductors and soloists we would like. Schedules are often more challenging, shorter rehearsal hours can lead to more sessions in a week with irregular days off.

There are always peaks and troughs in the life of any orchestra, principal conductors and CEOs come and go, each with their own style that suits us or not, as individuals or collectively. I tend to try to be optimistic through changes, though that's not always easy.

Camaraderie is of utmost importance, and good friends made at work are among the best. There are times when only other people who understand the stresses of the job at first hand can offer the right support. Touring is important for an orchestra, not only to make ourselves well known in distant places but for our bonding as a team. We tend to know the people who sit around us in our own sections the best, but on tours we end up getting to know more people.

I feel that some of the very best concerts I have taken part in have been while on tour, (and maybe one or two of the worst.... the less said....) and visiting so many places that I would never otherwise get to is a bonus.

Humour is a very important element in the life of a musician, and it often dispels tensions that accumulate in rehearsal or before nerve wracking concerts. We do tend to be quieter in rehearsals these days, much concentration is required, conductors tend to talk a bit more, and I would worry if our being able to laugh out loud at times was frowned upon, it is very necessary.

Although much is challenging in the job, when all the right elements come together there are moments when it all feels sublime. For me playing Richard Strauss Tone poems with Neeme Järvi, a conductor who could inspire you with minimal gestures was the ultimate. But from week to week, performing fantastic music with some extraordinary musicians - orchestra colleagues as well as soloists - can also produce spine tingling moments.

The thing that never changes for me is enjoyment of sharing the music with the audience. To hear a great piece of music for the first time is very special, even more so if it is performed live. I get a buzz from thinking about that, especially if it is a piece I have played hundreds of times, it makes me remember that feeling for myself. When you feel that the audience are with you….it doesn't get better than that.

Epilogue

The Price Of Fame

On the 10th September, 2016, the Scottish singer, KT Tunstall headlined at the BBC SSO's Proms in the Park concert, which has been held for the last few years on Glasgow Green. This yearly concert coincides with the Last night of the Proms in the RAH and is broadcast live on both BBC radio and television.

There are also simultaneous Proms in the Park concerts around the UK, in Belfast, Cardiff and London's Hyde Park, right opposite the Albert Hall, the venue for the actual Last Night, and in the second half of the concert, all these places link up live via the wonders of modern technology and perform a piece together.

KT, real name Kate, asked for three percussionists from the orchestra to join her, down at the front of the stage for a performance of one of her early hits, "Suddenly I See". Glynn Forrest - a tremendous player and immediately likeable chap, Dave and I obliged, and we did the number in my least favourite area of the concert platform - down at the front. I'm so much more comfortable at the back of the stage, but the whole thing went fine, luckily and there's even a clip of it on YouTube somewhere.

I loved KT's performance and she gave me the impression that she both knew exactly what she wanted and definitely knew what she was talking about, and I quickly became a fan of hers after that.

One of the highlights every year, for me, is someone who has become more or less one of the permanent fixtures of this prestigious evening, and also is the first call whenever the orchestra needs a bagpiper, even accompanying the BBC SSO on its most recent tour of China.

Chris Gibb obviously has a mate in every port because, when his Highland Dress for that tour went missing in transit, he nonchalantly phoned his pal in Hong Kong, who then drove across the Chinese border to Shenzhen, where the first concert was, and lent him his kilt.

The highlight in question for me is Chris' solo piping in "Highland Cathedral" and judging by the crowd's reaction every year when he walks onstage, playing, it's one of theirs too.

I was chatting with Chris at the break during the rehearsal, when he told me a great story about an unusual request McCallum Bagpipes received from the Middle East.

One of the world's leading bagpipe makers and based in Kilmarnock, they got a call from the Qatari army asking if they had anything to prevent their members from knocking their teeth out when they played the pipes while riding camels. The hard, wooden mouthpieces on the instruments had apparently become something of a dental problem, and so the Scottish pipe makers developed a flexible, bendy rubber mouthpiece for them.

Brilliant!

After the concert at Glasgow Green was over, us lot in the percussion section, packed up all the percussion gear into its flight cases as usual, for the short trip on Allan's instrument truck back to the City Halls.

By the time we finished, everyone else from the orchestra was long gone. There were, however quite a lot of other people still there, the day's work just beginning for some of them.

The de-rigging crew to dismantle the massive open-air stage, the tv crew packing up all their miles of cables and paraphernalia, and numerous folk from the sound and production teams were all still there and working away.

Tired and sweaty, I walked into the gent's band room, the only person there apart from a girl from the production team who was clearing everything away.

"Oh, sorry," she said. "I thought everyone had gone."

"That's ok," I replied. "I'm not getting changed, I'm just collecting my stuff and heading home."

The BBC had provided backstage snacks for the orchestra, and there were still quite a few left over. Boxes of crisps, hundreds of packets of Haribo sweets and large red, family-sized square plastic tubs of biscuits seemed to be the Corporation's idea of what musicians thought were healthy snacks.

"Would you like to take one of those biscuit tubs?" she asked me. "It's still unopened."

"Really? Is that allowed?" I didn't want to get myself or her into trouble for the heinous crime of stealing biscuits from the BBC.

"You were down the front with KT, weren't you?" she offered as qualification.

"Ah, fame at last," I joked.

She laughed and said "Absolutely," and pointing to the big red tub added, "And that's the price of fame."

"Free, leftover biscuits?"

"Yes, and they'll probably just get thrown out anyway."

"Haha! Thanks!"

I thought that was very nice of her.

I put a red plastic tub into my suit carrier, grabbed my stick bag and the rest of my gear, and left Glasgow Green, happy.

Happy because I was famous at last.

And if anyone doubted it, all I had to do was show them my biscuits to prove it.

So, in all honesty, I really did not think that thirty years after forcing myself to get that haircut and after the stress and pressure of that first *Alborada Del Grazioso* with the Scottish National Orchestra, I'd still be playing.

The stress and pressure are still there but now much more subdued, as are those fears of rejection and the times of having to deal with the actual rejection itself after unsuccessful auditions or whatever, but I'm a big boy now, so I can cope admirably.

There is still the dubious and erratic quality of many conductors which are big contributory factors to the stress and pressure, as I've previously mentioned once or twice already.

However, even after thirty years of all this, I still love what I do and I feel highly privileged to still be doing it.

I still love playing and can't ever imagine that changing, and I'm immensely lucky to be actually paid to be doing something I love and play my instrument(s) on a daily basis. I don't think I've ever woken up in the morning and thought "I really can't face work today…"

I have never lost sight of the fact that there is a long queue of eager players behind me who would jump at the chance to have the opportunities which I have had and continue to have, and this both keeps me on my toes and makes me appreciate all the more how lucky I am.

And anyway, the stress and pressure and all the other "bad" things about the profession really only help to make one a stronger, more resilient person and a better, more able musician. Eventually, I came to realise that it's a necessary part of the job we do, and I then found that by actually realising it, it makes everything a lot less difficult and daunting.

The people I've met over the years and the friends I've made in the world of music, both orchestral and non-orchestral have all made a great impact on me and will always be a huge part of me.

And that feeling of sitting on stage, being blasted by the backwards-facing bells of nine French horns during a Shostakovich symphony, right in the middle of the magnificent, immense wall of sound being produced by an orchestra of one hundred-plus top-class musicians is utterly staggering.

It's something that not many people in the overall scheme of things will ever get to experience, unfortunately.

I truly have an awesome job.

If you're a regular concert-goer then you'll know how amazing an experience hearing a live orchestra can be and I applaud you for your support of live orchestral music.

If you have been to a concert or an opera/ballet performance but not recently, then do go again - it just keeps getting better all the time.

If you've never been to one, and now that you know a lot more about it, I encourage you to go to an orchestral concert or an opera or a ballet. Google your nearest professional orchestra and buy a ticket, or better still, buy two tickets and take a friend. I guarantee you'll love it, and even more so if the programme includes any of the pieces mentioned in these pages.

And if it includes *The Firebird*, enjoy watching the audience briefly levitate and the bass drum player smile.

There's a question which I've been asked quite a few times recently;

If I had the chance, would I do it all over again, the good bits and the bad bits?

My answer is always the same.

Yes, of course I would.

Well, the good bits anyway.

Glossary

Abbreviations

BBC SO - British Broadcasting Corporation Symphony Orchestra

BBC SRO - BBC Scottish Radio Orchestra

BBC SSO - BBC Scottish Symphony Orchestra

CBSO - City of Birmingham Symphony Orchestra

ENO - English National Opera

GRCH - Glasgow Royal Concert Hall

HMT - His Majesty's Theatre, Aberdeen

LPO - London Philharmonic Orchestra

LSO - London Symphony Orchestra

NYCOS - National Youth Choir of Scotland

NYOS - National Youth Orchestra of Scotland

OSO - Orchestra of Scottish Opera

RAH - Royal Albert Hall, London

RCS - Royal Conservatoire of Scotland, formerly the RSAMD

RPO - Royal Philharmonic Orchestra

RSAMD - Royal Scottish Academy of Music and Drama (known affectionately as The Academy), now the Royal Conservatoire of Scotland

RSNO - Royal Scottish National Orchestra

SB - Scottish Ballet

SBO - Scottish Ballet Orchestra

SCO - Scottish Chamber Orchestra

SNO - Scottish National Orchestra. It received Royal status in 1991 and changed its name briefly to the Royal Scottish Orchestra before settling on Royal Scottish National Orchestra after public pressure.

SO - Scottish Opera

UO - Ulster Orchestra

UP - Usual Percussion (i.e. bass drum, snare drum, clash cymbals, suspended cymbal(s), triangle, tambourine, etc. - nothing exotic)

Musical terminology

(in general order of appearance)

piano - softly, quiet.

mezzo-forte - louder than *piano* (quiet) but quieter than *forte* (loud).

rallentando - a gradual slowing down.

forte-piano *(a musical direction)* - a note which starts with a loud attack and then is immediately soft (quiet).
   (Not to be confused with)

piano-forte (a musical instrument) - a *Joannah* on which one tinkles the ivories.

segue - A transition from one piece of music to another, without any break or interruption.

forte - loud.

double forte - very loud.

triple forte - new trousers, please.

crescendo - a gradual increase in loudness.

senza - without.

sforzando - with force, emphatically.

legato - in a smooth flowing manner, without breaks between notes.

staccato - a note of shortened duration; sharply detached or separated from the others.

pizzicato - On a stringed instrument, to pluck the string, as opposed to bowing it.

rubato -the temporary disregarding of strict tempo to allow a quickening or slackening of expression or rhythm.

anacrusis - a note or sequence of notes which precedes the first downbeat in a bar in a musical phrase.

tempo - the speed or pace of music.

Fencing terminology

Sporting Weapons

Foil - A fencing weapon with rectangular cross-section blade and a small bell guard. More generally, any sword that has been buttoned or had its point turned back to render it less dangerous for practice.

Épée - A fencing weapon with triangular cross-section blade and a large bell guard; also, a light duelling sword of similar design, popular in the mid-19th century, which was also called an 'Épée de Terrain'.

Sabre - A fencing weapon with a flat blade and knuckle guard, used with cutting or thrusting actions; a military sword popular in the 18th to 20th centuries; any cutting sword used by cavalry. The modern fencing sabre is descended from the duelling sabre of Italy and Germany, which was straight and thin with sharp edges, but had a blunt point.

General Fencing Terminology Used Within This Book

(In order of appearance)

en guard - French for "on guard"; spoken at outset to warn the participants to take a defensive position.

feint - An offensive movement resembling an attack in all but its continuance. It is an attack into one line with the intention of switching to another line before the attack is completed. A feint is intended to draw a reaction from an opponent. This is the 'intention', and the reaction is generally a parry, which can then be deceived.

sixte - area of the upper quarter of the body on the side closest to the sword arm.

counter-disengage - A type of *feint*. Disengages are usually executed in conjunction with an extension/attack, though technically, they are just a deception around the opponent's blade. To use in an attack, *feint* an attack with an extension and avoid the opponent's attempt to parry or press your blade, using as small a circular motion as possible. Circle under the opponent's blade. The first extension must be a believable *feint* in order to draw a reaction. Be prepared to proceed forward with a straight attack if no parry response is forthcoming.

attack au fer - An attack on the opponent's blade, e.g. beat, expulsion, pressure.

lunge - The most basic and common attacking movement in modern fencing. This description adheres basically to the French school of fencing, and describes the legwork involved. The actions of the hand/arm/blade are considered separately from this discussion. From *en garde*, push the front heel out by extending the front leg from the knee. Do not bend the front ankle or lift up on the ball of the front foot. This means that the front foot must move forward prior to the body weight shifting forward. As the front leg extends, energetically push erect body forward with the rear leg. Rear arm extends during forward motion as a counterbalance. Land on the front heel and glide down into final position, with front shin perpendicular to the ground, and both heels on the floor. During this action, the torso should remain relatively erect, and not be thrown forward. Often, the back foot can be pulled along behind during an energetic lunge. It is important, and a fundamental characteristic of the lunge, to fully extend the back leg, obtaining full power from this spring-like extension. Aldo Nadi, of the Italian school of fencing, wrote an extensive description of how the lunge should be executed.

flèche - Flèche means 'arrow' in French. The rear leg is brought in front of the front leg and the fencer sprints past his/her opponent. This action is currently not allowed during sabre bouts, because the front and rear legs must not cross. In épée, a quick pass is essential, since the defending fencer is allowed one attack after the pass, so long as the defenders attack is in one action, with or without a parry, initiated before the pass is completed.

quarte - area of the upper quarter of the body on the side furthest from the sword arm.

balestra - A footwork preparation, consisting of a jump forwards. It is most often, but not always, immediately followed by a lunge. It is faster than an advance forward, which helps change the rhythm and timing of moves. 'Balestra' is the French term for sudden leap.

foible - the flexible, weaker half of the blade further away from the *hilt*. The other, stronger half is the *forte*.

phrase -a sequence of fencing movements performed without a break.

parry -A simple defensive action designed to deflect an attack, performed with the forte of the blade. A parry is usually only wide enough to allow the attacker's blade to just miss; any additional motion is wasteful. A well-executed parry should take the foible of the attacker's blade with the forte and/or guard of the defender's. This provides the greatest control over the opponent's blade. In sabre, the guard should be turned appropriately using the fingers to protect the wrist. Parries generally cover one of the 'lines' of the body. The simplest parries move the blade in a straight line. Other parries move the blade in a circular, semi-circular, or diagonal manner. There are eight basic parries, and many derivatives of these eight. (see #Prime, #Seconde, #Tierce, #Quarte, #Quinte, #Sixte, #Septime, #Octave, #Neuvieme). See also 'Lines'. In foil, the opponent's blade should not only be deflected away from the target, but away from off-target areas as well. An attack that is deflected off the valid target but onto invalid target still retains right-of-way. In sabre, the opponent's blade need only be deflected away from valid target, since off-target touches do not stop the phrase. Sabre parries must be particularly clean and clear to avoid the possibility of whip-over touches. In épée, a good parry is simply any one that gains enough time for the riposte; opposition parries and *prise-de-fer* are commonly used, since they do not release the opponent's blade to allow a *remise*.

prise-de-fer - (French: Literally "take the steel"); also "Taking the Blade"; an engagement of the blades that attempts to control the opponent's weapon. See also #Beat, #Press, #Expulsion, #Bind, #Croisé, #Envelopment, #Opposition, #Transfer.

remise - An immediate, direct replacement of an attack that missed, was short, or was parried, without withdrawing the arm. A remise is a direct continuation, meaning that no deceptions or changes of line occur with the continuation (replacement) of the attack. In foil and sabre, a remise does not have right of way over an immediate riposte. See also #Renewal, #Reprise and #Redoublement.

(Note: These are only the fencing terms I've used in this book - there are a LOT more.... I did say the rules were complex!)

Related Listening

All the artists/composers/works mentioned or alluded to in the preceding pages, in general order of appearance.

Nutville - **The Buddy Rich Big Band**

Falling Knives - **Voodoo Six**

God Only Knows - **The Beach Boys**

American Trilogy - **Elvis**

While My Guitar Gently Weeps - **The Beatles**

Hot for Teacher - **Van Halen**

Love Hurts - **Nazareth**

Raintown - **Deacon Blue**

Tears of a Clown - **Smokey Robinson**

Stay With Me - **The Faces**

Raise Your Hands - **Bon Jovi**

Last in Line - **Dio**

Neon Knights - **Black Sabbath**

Gates of Babylon - **Rainbow**

Battle Hymns - **Manowar**

Distant Early Warning - **Rush**

Angels of War - **Crimson Glory**

Roundabout - **Yes**

London - **Queensrÿche**

Rime of the Ancient Mariner - **Iron Maiden**

The Hellion/Screaming for Vengeance - **Judas Priest**

747 (Strangers in the Night) - **Saxon**

Rock of Ages - **Def Leppard**

Bomber - **Motörhead**

Breakout - **Glasgow**

Alborada Del Grazioso - **Maurice Ravel**

Scheherazade - **Nikolai Rimsky-Korsakov**

Der Prince von Homburg - **Hans Werner Henze**

Alexander Nevsky - **Sergei Prokofiev**

Swan Lake - **Pyotr Ilyich Tchaikovsky**

Who Cares? - **George Gershwin**

Fantasy Overture 'Romeo and Juliet' - **Pyotr Ilyich Tchaikovsky**

Rhapsody on a theme of Paganini - **Sergei Rachmaninov**

Orchestral Theatre I: Xun - **Tan Dun**

Symphony No. 9 in E flat major - **Dmitri Shostakovich**

Carmina Burana - **Carl Orff**

Don Juan - **Richard Strauss**

Farandole - **Georges Bizet**

The Firebird - **Igor Stravinsky**

By The Beautiful Blue Danube - **Johann Strauss II**

Petrushka - **Igor Stravinsky**

Short Ride in a Fast Machine - **John Adams**

Crazy Horses - **The Osmonds**

Cinderella - **Sergei Prokofiev**

Romeo and Juliet - **Sergei Prokofiev**

La Fille Mal Gardée - **Ferdinand Hérold/John Lanchberry**

Napoli - **Edvard Helsted, Holger Simon Paulli, Niels W. Gade, François Henri Prume, Hans Christian Lumbye**

Coppelia - **Léo Delibes**

La Sylphide - **Herman Severin Løvenskiold**

Sleeping Beauty - **Pyotr Ilyich Tchaikovsky**

The Nutcracker - **Pyotr Ilyich Tchaikovsky**

Peter and the Wolf - **Sergei Prokofiev**

Giselle - **Adolphe Charles Adam**

Within the Quota - **Cole Porter**

Symphony Op. 21 - **Anton Webern**

Sinfonia da Requiem - **Benjamin Britten**

Peter Pan - **Eddie McGuire**

A Streetcar Named Desire - **Peter Salem**

32 Cryptograms - **Robert Moran**

Two Pigeons - **André Messager/John Lanchberry**

Lincoln Portrait - **Aaron Copland**

Symphony no. 5 - **Ludwig van Beethoven**

L'Histoire du Soldat - **Igor Stravinsky**

Symphony No. 3 - **Michael Tippet**

Chronochromie - **Olivier Messiaen**

Ionisation - **Edgard Varèse**

Sad Jane - **Frank Zappa/LSO**

Purple Haze - **Jimi Hendrix**

Enter Sandman - **Metallica**

Black Rose - **Thin Lizzy**

Whole Lotta love - **Led Zeppelin**

Are You Gonna Go My Way? - **Lenny Kravitz**

Wishing Well - **Free**

Keep on Rocking in the Free World - **Neil Young**

Whipping Post - **Allman Brothers/Frank Zappa**

Stonehenge - **Spinal Tap**

Let There Be Rock - **AC/DC**

Those Magnificent Men in Their Flying Machines - **Ron Goodwin**

Belshazzar's Feast - **William Walton**

Local Boy in the Photograph - **Stereophonics**

Kiss - **Prince**

Especially For You - **Kylie Minogue and Jason Donovan**

Baby, I Love You - **The Ramones**

Symphony Fantastique - **Hector Berlioz**

The Last Supper - **Harrison Birtwhistle**

Taverner - **Peter Maxwell Davies**

Symphony No. 9 - **Gustav Mahler**

Pelléas et Mélisande - **Claude Debussy**

Wozzeck - **Alban Berg**

Der Rosenkavalier - **Richard Strauss**

Suddenly I See - **KT Tunstall**

Highland Cathedral - **Ulrich Roever and Michael Korb**

Symphony No. 7 in C major - **Dmitri Shostakovich**

Sources

The World-Wide Interweb, including

(1) theatrestrust.org.uk

heraldscotland.com

britishfencing.com

bpa.org.uk (British Parachute Association)

Rumor of War – Philip Caputo (Pimlico, 1999)

Scottish Ballet: Forty Years - Mary Brennan (Saraband, 2009)

Acknowledgements

Thank you,

My parents, Margaret and Martin for everything.

Anne Brincourt, for all your support and encouragement and for your excellent proof reading and editorial skills.

For help of all kinds, from answering my weird and random questions, oblivious of my ulterior motives, to providing various contact details, and for great support, even if you were unaware of it:

Joan Morrison, Eddie Gallagher, Simon Johnson, Eldon Byrne, Ewen Mackay, Terry Johns, Ian Budd, Julia Norton, Mireia Ferrer, Nigel Mason, Alan Friel, Brian McGinley, John Kazek, Asher Zaccardelli, Ana Cordova Andres, Miranda Phythian-Adams, Scott Lumsdaine, Alastair Savage, Chris Gibb and Chris Terian.

For their kindness and outstanding contributions to this book, Allan Hannah, Jane Reid, Robert Baxter, Richard Honner, Martyn Brabbins, John Gracie and Ralph Tartaglia.

For pointing me in the right direction, Luke Brown. Check out Luke's fantastic first novel, "My Biggest Lie" (Cannongate, 2014).

For excellent publishing advice and encouragement, the supremely multi-talented John K. Irvine. I wholly recommend John's novel trilogy, "The Smith Chronicles", and also his studio albums "Wait & See" and "Next Stop".

Kit Foster for creating such a brilliant cover.

Janice Bell at The Herald for kind permission to use the article in *Certa Cito.*

The small handful of individuals who knew about this project and kept the whole thing quiet – you know who you are and I knew I could trust you.

About the Author

Martin Willis was born in Glasgow, Scotland where he still lives and gets on really well with his neighbours, mainly because he doesn't practice at home. This is his first book.

Made in the USA
Columbia, SC
28 July 2018